GRIZZLY BEARS

GRIZZLY BEARS

Text and Photographic Selection by

CANDACE SAVAGE

Foreword by Andy Russell

Sierra Club Books
San Francisco

The Sierra Club, founded in 1892 by John Muir, has devoted itself to the study and protection of the earth's scenic and ecological resources—mountains, wetlands, woodlands, wild shores and rivers, deserts and plains. The publishing program of the Sierra Club offers books to the public as a nonprofit educational service in the hope that they may enlarge the public's understanding of the Club's basic concerns. The point of view expressed in each book, however, does not necessarily represent that of the Club. The Sierra Club has some sixty chapters coast to coast, in Canada, Hawaii, and Alaska. For information about how you may participate in its programs to preserve wilderness and the quality of life, please address inquiries to Sierra Club, 730 Polk Street, San Francisco, Ca 94109.

Originally published in Canada by Douglas & McIntyre Ltd., 1615 Venables Street, Vancouver, British Columbia, Canada V5L 2H1.

Library of Congress Cataloging-in-Publication Data
Savage, Candace, 1949-
    Grizzly bears / text and photographic selection by Candace
    Savage; foreword by Andy Russell.
        p.   cm.
    ISBN 0-87156-633-8
    1. Grizzly bear.   I. Title.
QA 737.C27S265   1990
599.74'446--dc20   90-8348
                                       CIP

The following publishers have given permission to use quoted material:
From *Men for the Mountains* by Sid Marty. Copyright © 1978 by Sid Marty. Reprinted by permission of the Canadian Publishers, McClelland and Stewart, Toronto. From *The Sacred Paw* by Paul Shepard and Barry Sanders. Copyright © 1985 by Paul Shepard and Barry Sanders. Reprinted by permission of Viking/Penguin. From "The Ark of the Mind" by Paul Shepard in *Parabola* 8(2). Copyright © 1983 by Paul Shepard. Reprinted by permission of Paul Shepard. From "Aspects of Evolution and Adaptation in Bears of North America" by Stephen Herrero in *Bears—Their Biology and Management*, edited by Stephen Herrero. Copyright © 1972 by IUCN, Morges, Switzerland. Reprinted by permission of IUCN. From *Bear Attacks: Their Causes and Avoidance* by Stephen Herrero. Copyright © 1985 by Stephen Herrero. Reprinted by permission of Nick Lyons Books. From *The Grizzlies of Mount McKinley* by Adolph Murie. Copyright © 1981. Reprinted by permission of the U.S. Department of the Interior, National Park Service, Washington, D.C. From "Do Carnivores Have a Future?" by Monte Hummel in *Bear-People Conflicts*, edited by Marianne Bromley. Copyright © 1989. Reprinted by permission of Monte Hummel, World Wildlife Fund. From "'Grizz': Of Men and the Great Bear" by Douglas H. Chadwick in *National Geographic* 69 (2). Copyright © 1986 by the National Geographic Society. Reprinted by permission of the National Geographic Society. From *Grizzly Country* by Andy Russell. Copyright © 1967 by Andy Russell. Reprinted by permission of Alfred A. Knopf. From "Reproductive Biology of Female Brown Bears (*Ursos arctos*), McNeil River, Alaska" by L. P. Glenn, J. W. Lentfer, J. B. Faro and L. H. Miller in *Bears—Their Biology and Management*. Copyright © 1976 by IUCN, Morges, Switzerland. Reprinted by permission of IUCN. From *A Sand County Almanac* by Aldo Leopold. Copyright © 1949, 1973, by Aldo Leopold. Reprinted by permission of Oxford University Press. From "The Conservation Ethic" by Aldo Leopold in *Journal of Forestry* (October 1933; reprinted in June 1989). Copyright © 1933, 1989, by the Society of American Foresters. Reprinted by permission of the Society of American Foresters. From "The Hunter, the Games, and the Unseen Powers: Lappish and Finnish Bear Rites" by Carl-Martin Edsman in *Hunting and Fishing*, edited by Harald Hvarfner. Copyright © 1965. Reprinted by permission of Norbottens Museum, Stockholm. From "Bear Mother" by Marius Barbeau in *Journal of American Folklore* 59 (231). Copyright © 1945. Reprinted by permission of the American Folklore Society. Not for sale or further reproduction. From "The Last Stronghold of the Grizzly" by J.W. Schoen, S.D. Miller, and H.V. Reynolds III in *Natural History* 96:50–60. Copyright © 1987 by the American Museum of Natural History. Reprinted by permission of the American Museum of Natural History.

Design by Alexandra Hass
Front jacket photograph by Art Wolfe
Back jacket photograph by Karl Sommerer
Maps by Lisa Ireton
Typeset by The Typeworks
Printed and bound in Singapore by C. S. Graphics Pte. Ltd.

10 9 8 7 6 5 4 3 2 1

CONTENTS

For my mother, Edna Sherk,
who taught me how to write

For my father, Harry Sherk,
who showed me how to care

ACKNOWLEDGEMENTS

This book rests on the work of two generations of scholars and scientists. In particular, I would like to acknowledge my debt to those with whom I spoke or met during my research. They include:

Ralph Archibald, British Columbia Ministry of Environment ■ Larry Aumiller, Alaska Department of Fish and Game ■ Claude Berducou, Office National des Fôrets, France ■ George Blondin, Dene Cultural Institute ■ Peter Clarkson, Northwest Territories Department of Renewable Resources ■ John Gunson, Alberta Forestry, Lands and Wildlife ■ Tony Hamilton, British Columbia Ministry of Environment ■ Stephen Herrero, University of Calgary and IUCN/SCC Bear Specialist Group ■ Wayne McCrory, McCrory Wildlife Services ■ Bruce McLelland, British Columbia Ministry of Environment ■ Harry Reynolds III, Alaska Department of Fish and Game ■ John Schoen, Alaska Department of Fish and Game ■ Christopher Servheen, U.S. Grizzly Bear Recovery Coordinator and IUCN/SCC Bear Specialist Group Barney Smith, Yukon Department of Renewable Resources ■ Mitch Taylor, Northwest Territories Department of Renewable Resources ■

I owe a particular debt to Stephen Herrero, Christopher Servheen and Barney Smith for reviewing the manuscript, and to Christopher Servheen and Peter Clarkson for assistance with the distribution maps. Any remaining inadequacies in the text are, of course, entirely my own responsibility.

The staffs of the Yellowknife Public Library, the Renewable Resources Library and the N.W.T. Government Library provided superb support—especially Vera Raschke. Credit is also due to Cam Cathcart of Vancouver for the suggestion that led to this book, and to Rob Sanders, Alex Hass and Nancy Flight for collaborating with me to make it a reality.

Last but certainly not least, it is a joy to acknowledge the gentle and generous support of my daughter, Diana Savage, and my friend Richard Clarke.

FOREWORD

*bout seventy years ago, my father showed me a big grizzly track imprinted in wet silt near a little spring. The track was so fresh that the water was welling up in it. I was not afraid, for my father did nothing to make me so, but I distinctly recall a deep feeling of awe at the size of the track.*

Having spent the greater part of my life living and rambling around in grizzly country, I have encountered grizzlies countless times since then. Sometimes they were so close I could smell them. I have hunted them, though I have killed very few. I have spent innumerable hours watching them in complete fascination and learning about their habits, their likes and their dislikes.

Grizzlies are big, powerful and quick to move. They are also highly intelligent. They have superlative noses and excellent ears, though their vision is less than razor sharp. No two grizzlies are the same; they are just as different from each other as people are. But they all have one thing in common: they are very honest. Step over their line of tolerance, and they let you know about it in an instant.

Many people are afraid of grizzlies. People who are afraid suffer from a chronic apprehension that takes a great deal of the pleasure out of travelling through bear country. This fear can turn into sheer panic when they meet a grizzly at close range, and a very dangerous encounter can result.

In contrast, some people have learned merely to be scared of grizzlies on occasion. These people manage to get around in grizzly country without undue worry by keeping their eyes open and taking a few sensible precautions. They may become scared when they meet a bear, but they remain in full control of the situation by moving carefully and avoiding perilous contact. Rather than reacting frantically, which can be disastrous, they stay in command of themselves.

Grizzlies dislike being surprised at close quarters. In fact, 90 per cent of them will do everything possible to avoid close-range contact with humans, even in national parks, where they enjoy full protection and know they have nothing to fear from firearms.

My wife and I raised five children with no casualties, though it was not unusual for grizzlies to wander through our yard. Often, if we had not seen their tracks, we would not have known they had been there. One summer, a couple of young photographers and I travelled through some of the best grizzly habitat left in the world without seeing a single bear.

Over two seasons, my two oldest sons, Dick and Charlie, and I made a movie featuring the grizzly and associated species. We found them difficult subjects because they usually kept hidden in brush and timber. After the first season, we stopped carrying guns while we were filming, for somehow bears know if a person is armed. Altogether, we made 202 close-range approaches to the bears and shot three hundred metres (a thousand feet) of film. Sometimes they tolerated our presence at very close range without even acknowledging our presence, though we were in plain sight. We enjoyed some golden hours filming those bears.

On about a dozen occasions, however, we faced angry charges when we did something wrong, like staying beyond our welcome or moving erratically or just being in the wrong place at the right time. We had one rule for such occasions; we planted our feet and faced the bears. They expected us to run, as everything does from a griz-

zly. When we didn't, they always stopped or veered away. If we moved at all, it was generally towards them. Once when Dick and I were charged by a mother with two almost full grown cubs, we stopped them at about six metres (twenty feet) across a narrow ravine and then carefully backed off to one side to give them room to go up it. Grizzlies hate to lose face by backing off, and these bears chose to take a side track up onto a hidden bench, where they started feeding again. We quietly and diplomatically removed ourselves from the immediate vicinity with heartfelt sighs of relief. Grizzlies are never boring!

The text and photographs on the following pages dispel many of the common misconceptions about grizzly bears and contribute a great deal to our understanding of these honest and intelligent animals. Not only have the photographers mastered their equipment, the vagaries of light and the magic of modern film, but they have also attained a real understanding of a very difficult subject. They are brave but not reckless, realizing that grizzlies do not brook a great deal of error.

Such naturalist-photographers are probably the best friends that the bears have found among people, for they know that grizzlies have a large measure of tolerance and can generally be trusted so long as their environmental boundaries are respected. The photographers whose work is represented on these pages, along with the author of this book, are educating those of us who do not have the opportunity to learn the truth in any other way.

Andy Russell

GRIZZLY BEARS

RICK MCINTYRE

THE POWER OF THE BEAR

"*he reason that grizzlies are not extinct is that they have power.*"

George Blondin is known among the Dene of the Northwest Territories as an elder, a term that honours wisdom as well as age. A robust man in his sixties, he sits at a plain desk in a bare-walled basement office. Outside the high window are rows of parked cars and the snow-hushed bustle of northern city life. But George Blondin is not of the city, and as he talks, his mind travels the land and rivers near Great Bear Lake, the country of his youth.

"I mean mental power. Bears use it to turn people away, to keep hunters from killing them in their dens. Otherwise, they would all have been shot."

There was the time, he recalls, when a visitor (not an Indian) went on a winter bear hunt with a Dene father and son. When they found a grizzly in a den, the visitor brashly predicted that they would all be eating bear the next day. The Dene warned him not to be crude. You can't talk bluntly about "eating bear"; you must use terms of respect. But the visitor went on prattling.

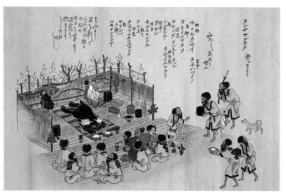

The Ainu, the aboriginal people of Hokkaido in northern Japan, performed an elaborate ritual in which a captive grizzly was killed and "sent away" to the gods with gifts from humankind. Top, *the bear is borne in for the ceremony;* bottom, *the "visitor," now dead, is offered food as a token of good will. These scrolls were painted in the 1840s.*
THE BROOKLYN MUSEUM

Next morning, when he and the hunters went back to claim their prize, the father and son took turns poking a stick in the den to rouse the dormant bear. They stood back, tense, waiting for the animal to emerge. Nothing happened. Again they prodded. Still nothing. Finally, one after the other, they crawled gingerly into the cavity. The grizzly was not there; it had taken offense and disappeared.

Blondin offers this story as proof that bears have powers of understanding. They are the only animals, he says, who can read our thoughts and understand human speech.

He remembers that his father spoke to every bear he met. "Grandfather," he would say, "we don't mean you any harm. Please don't hurt us. Let us go our way and bring us luck on our hunt." The grizzly, hearing these calm words and honourable intentions, would turn and walk away. "If you speak from the heart," Blondin maintains, "bears will understand." He knows; he is speaking from experience.

Among all these wonders, what impresses him most about grizzlies is their ability to hibernate. Each fall, when the roots and berries on which they rely for food wither in the cold, grizzly bears dig dens in the ground, curl up inside and wait for winter to pass. For as long as seven months, they do not eat, drink or pass wastes. When they emerge in the spring, they return again to regular life, as if they have been reborn. Some of the females come out of their dens with tiny cubs, born while the mothers slept. Birth and rebirth in one.

"It's amazing," Blondin says, shaking his head. "How can any animal do that?"

One theory, which he remembers from the elders of his youth, is that hibernating bears nourish themselves by sucking fat through their paws. This is an odd idea and at first hearing may seem of no great significance. But to encounter it here, in a drab office, in the last decade of the twentieth century, is a jolt. Anthropologists think this belief is well over ten thousand years old. By its very oddity, this homely scrap of folklore serves as a "tag" that helps identify a rich complex of practices and beliefs that span three continents and more than a hundred centuries.

The vision of the grizzly that George Blondin articulates was once common across Eurasia and North America, from Scandinavia to Japan, over the Bering Strait, south to the Columbia River and east to Labrador. Until very recently, bear rites, some simple, some complex, were practised by many of the traditional peoples of the Northern Hemisphere: the Saamis.(Lapps), Finns, Ostyak, Olcha, Vogul, Gilyak, Ainu, Tsimshian, Haida, Tlingit, Slavey, Cree, Ojibwa, Micmac, Delaware and others. Although no two of these cults were exactly alike, they were linked by similar beliefs, customs and purposes. Scholars believe that these cults originated among ancient Asian hunters, whose descendants brought them to North America at the end of the Ice Age, or earlier still, among the ancient people who honoured cave bears.

As Swedish anthropologist Carl-Martin Edsman

The Greek heroine Callisto watches her hand turn into the paw of a bear. Fully transformed, Callisto was later transported to the heavens, where she became Ursa Major, the Great Bear. This vase dates from the fourth century B.C.
THE J. PAUL GETTY MUSEUM

points out, "Remarkable finds of ritually buried bear skulls and bones in stone-age caves in the Alpine region and the South of France present great resemblances with rites still observed among the northern hunting peoples, and thus testify to the age of these ceremonies and the conceptions corresponding to them."

In its time, the cave bear, *Ursus spelaeus,* was "the most bearish of bears," ferocious and huge, and may have been hunted and honoured by humankind for forty thousand years. But when it became extinct, about ten thousand years ago, the veneration passed to other bears, especially the grizzly, *Ursus arctos.** The most widely distributed species of bear in the world, the grizzly—or brown bear, as it is also known—spans the world of the bear ceremonies.

▶*Ursus arctos* is known by different names in different parts of the world. In Europe and areas of Alaska, the species is known as the brown bear, but in the rest of North America, it is called the grizzly. Other terms, such as *higuma,* red bear and horse bear, are used in Japan, India and Tibet. To avoid the awkwardness of composite names, such as grizzly/brown bear, the word *grizzly* is used here in an expanded sense to refer to all races of *Ursus arctos,* wherever they occur.

This covered gold dish by Haida artist Bill Reid honours the inspiration of the Bear Mother myth. Here, Bear Mother nurses her twin cubs.
THE NATIONAL MUSEUM OF CANADA

At the heart of the ceremonies, scholars say, there lies a myth, perhaps inspired by grizzlies and certainly of great antiquity. We glimpse it in figurines made in Yugoslavia and Greece during the New Stone Age, seven thousand years ago— miniature terra-cotta statues of a goddess with the head of a bear, nursing a bear cub. It is echoed in Slavic birth customs that identify a new mother as "the bear" and in the festival of Panagia Arkoudiotissa, "Virgin Mary of the Bear," which is celebrated on the second day of February at a cave in western Crete. We remember it clearly in stories that are still sometimes told in Sweden, Finland, Siberia and Canada. Of these, the version from the British Columbia coast, as recorded by anthropologist Marius Barbeau, is the best known.

It seems that long ago, there was a young girl named Peesunt who often went into the mountains with her friends to pick huckleberries. But instead of singing to warn the bears of her presence, as she should have done, she chatted and laughed disrespectfully. One day, when she and her friends were returning home with heavy baskets of fruit, Peesunt's pack strap broke and she

was left behind. Evening fell, and out of the darkness came two young men, "looking like brothers," who offered to help.

As she followed them up the mountain, Peesunt noticed that they were wearing bear robes. They led her to their home where several other people, dressed in the same way, sat around a fire. "The white mouse Tseets—Grandmother—came to her and pulled at her robe, which was now coated with long grey hair like a bear's. And the mouse squeaked, 'Granddaughter, the bears have taken you to their den; from now on you shall be one of them, bearing children.'" Peesunt became the wife of one of the spirit bears and bore twins, who were half human and half grizzly.

All this time, Peesunt's human brothers were searching for her. Eventually, they located her, climbed up to the den and killed her bear husband. Before he died, the bear taught his wife two ritual songs, "which the hunters should use over his dead body," to ensure good fortune. Peesunt's sons became expert bear hunters, and through their help and the protection of the dirge songs, she and her people prospered.

Peesunt is the Bear Mother, the "sacred virgin" of the Saamis, who overcomes the division between human and animal, matter and spirit, profane and divine. Through her, the people receive the skills and ritual knowledge they need to ensure that grizzlies and other animals will come back to them and permit themselves to be hunted. By honouring the grizzly bear as they have been taught, the people will survive.

In Swedish, courtship or betrothal is still sometimes spoken of as "bear-capture," in distant remembrance, perhaps, of the Bear Mother and of a time when each new human family reenacted the sacred compact of the mythic bear marriage. We allude to the bear too in our words for motherhood, through the Old European root *bher* and the Germanic *beran*, which mean "to bear children," the Germanic *barnum* ("bairn," or "child"), the Old Norse *burdh* ("birth").

Among the Ainu, the aboriginal people of northern Japan, women sometimes acted on these associations by nursing and rearing young bears. In their culture, well into the twentieth century, this was the first step of preparation for an elaborate ceremony called *Iyomante*, or "sending home," in which grizzly bears were honoured as intermediaries with god. (The grizzly is "frightening, unpredictable, gentle, intelligent, awe-inspiring, dangerous, and beautiful—like God," Canadian writer Sid Marty says, echoing the Ainu insight. "Maybe it is God, or one expression of Him.")

As part of the ritual, the captive cub was killed, for the Ainu observed that the god must die in order to be reborn. Later the bears' flesh was shared as a feast by members of the community. In their book *The Sacred Paw: The Bear in Nature, Myth and Literature*, Paul Shepard and Barry Sanders identify this as a form of sacrament: "To be joined with the god was experienced first—and continues to be most deeply felt—in the eating of the sacred body."

Wherever they are found in the Northern Hemisphere, bear ceremonies acknowledge and invoke the deep, contrasting emotions that grizzlies arouse. They speak of kinship and cordiality, for the slain bear is welcomed as an honoured guest. They speak of fear, for even in death, the grizzlies'

At the climax of the Bear Mother story, the bear husband is killed by his wife's brother (right). In this traditional Haida carving, the dying bear clings to his human wife.
ROYAL BRITISH COLUMBIA MUSEUM

anger must be deflected or atoned. They speak of respect, for when the bear's body has been ceremonially consumed, its bones are often buried with care and reverence. In this way, it is believed, the grizzly bear will be reborn and come to the hunters again.

The bear will be reborn—as it is reborn each spring from its den, as nature is reborn from the cold of winter, as humans may hope for rebirth from the cold of death.

The grizzly stands at the centre of the spiral of life. People "have always suspected that certain animals are masters and keepers of important secrets," Paul Shepard says; the bear guards the secret of renewal. Overhead by night, the celestial bears write their cyclic message across northern skies. Two clusters of bright stars dominate the heavens in the Northern Hemisphere. Sometimes identified as the Big and Little Dippers, they are known in classical mythology as the Great Bear, Ursa Major, and the Little Bear, Ursa Minor. As the story is usually told, the Great Bear is identified with the nymph Callisto, who was turned into a bear as a punishment for committing adultery with Zeus. The Little Bear is her son,

Two hunters in the Rocky Mountains rest with the trophies of a single day's hunt, 1910. Excessive shooting is largely to blame for the long-term decline in the population and range of grizzly bears throughout the Northern Hemisphere.
BYRON HARMON, WHYTE MUSEUM OF THE CANADIAN
ROCKIES, BANFF, ALBERTA

Arkas, the founding hero of Arkadia, the wild, mountainous interior of the Peloponnese. But it seems unlikely that the tale has come to us in its original form. Callisto, after all, is a woman-in-the-form-of-a-bear who, like the Bear Mother, made love with a god and, through her son, secured the future of her race. Her name is an

epithet of Artemis, the bear goddess, in whose honour Athenian girls once masked and danced as bears. Surely, her position in the heavens is an honorary one, and not a sign of disgrace.

The Greeks were not the only group to position the bear at the centre of the night. To the Iroquois and the Micmac, some of these same stars revealed a bear pursued by seven hunters, whereas the Hindus counted out seven bears. In these traditions and others, the bear stars hold the centre of the whirling firmament. The polestar, the hub around which the heavens turn, is the end of the Little Bear's tail, and the Great Bear, close by, offers sighting lines by which it can be found. To this day, we use it to get our "bearings" when we are lost.

Night by night, the heavenly bears draw the stars behind them, ushering in each new day. According to Hindu mythology, they are the whirlwind at the heart of the universe, the force that turns the life-giving wheel of the year. "The Great Bear is the ever-turning mandala in the sky," Shepard and Sanders say, and "the Pole Star... provides more than mere navigational guidance—serving as the still center of the wheel, offering spiritual bearings for the religious wanderer."

Grizzly bears have meaning for people; they burn bright in the human mind. Even today, alienated as we are from the natural world, we can sense their power. A few decades ago, when roadside feeding of bears was permitted in several North American parks, people poured in by the thousands. Many of them were deliriously unwary—offering food from bare fingers and lifting their children onto the animals' backs. In a way that defies reason, we trust bears and want to be close to them.

Similar yearnings may help account for the phenomenal success of the teddy bear. Why should it be that we entrust our children to the comfort of toy bears? Across Europe and North America, millions of one-eyed, threadbare teddies (or Pad-

dingtons or Poohs) work their magic every night. The teddy bear, or Teddy's bear, as it was originally called, was created in 1902 by a media event. In November of that year, U.S. president Theodore Roosevelt went to Mississippi to help settle a boundary dispute. As a break from the negotiations, he went out hunting but had no success. So someone produced a bedraggled little bear cub on a lead and suggested that Roosevelt might like to shoot it. Roosevelt, to his credit, declined. "I draw the line," he said. "If I shot that little fellow, I couldn't look my own boys in the face again." A cartoonist with the *Washington Post* used the event to satire the political negotiations, during which Roosevelt had also "drawn the line" at using his presidential powers to settle the dispute.

This image—the tough Rough Rider standing beside the spared cub—was widely publicized. Its political overtones were quickly forgotten, but the little bear was an instant success. The lovable, huggable bear-cub toy was put on the market in North America and Europe the following year, where it exerted a prompt and enduring appeal on adults and children alike. In twentieth-century culture, the teddy has virtually achieved the status of talisman, a protector against disorder and things that go bump in the night.

But our conception of the grizzly also has a darker side—a nightmare bear with glinting fangs and fiery eyes. Like our trust of bears, our terror is often extravagant. Grizzlies do kill people; that is beyond dispute. But such events are surprisingly rare. In North America, for example, visitors to mountain parks are more likely to be struck by lightning than to be killed by a grizzly bear. Yet a decade ago, when two campers were killed by

A pair of village entertainers in present-day Yugoslavia. Training grizzlies as performers is a longstanding tradition in many parts of Europe.
ALOJZIJE FRKOVIC

Romans, for their part, enrolled bears as gladiators in public spectacles. In A.D. 237, one thousand grizzlies are said to have been slaughtered in a single day. When the local supply of bears was exterminated, the emperors sent to North Africa for fighting stock, perhaps contributing to the eventual extinction of the African grizzly as well.

By the Middle Ages, such bloody entertainments had evolved into bearbaiting, a sport that remained popular in Europe for several centuries. In a typical bout, the grizzly was beaten, blinded and tied to a post in the centre of a bearbaiting pit. Dogs and men with whips were then turned loose on it, and onlookers hooted and cheered as it tried to defend itself. Sometimes, for the further edification of the crowd, the bear was identified with the devil or a deadly sin, to be vanquished by a determined assault.

On the American frontier, such superficial allegories were not found necessary. Unabashed prize fights between grizzlies and Spanish bulls were enjoyed by Californians through most of the nineteenth century. Sometimes the bears, careless of their reputation for ferocity, refused to fight until they were goaded with nails on the end of sticks, but usually they stood their ground and met their opponents head on. Strength met strength: the grizzly slashed with tooth and claw; the bull tore flesh with its sharp horns; and one or the other of the animals was eventually killed. These vicious spectacles were no doubt deeply satisfying to frontiersmen because they proved that taming the wilderness was a godly and essential task. Who would wish to share their land with such gruesome beasts? The California grizzly was extinct by 1922.

grizzlies in Glacier National Park, the tragedy was distended into the plot of a horror film: "Eighteen feet of gut-crunching, man-eating terror!" the marquees trumpeted.

Our ancestors exploited similar feelings, and even the ancient bear ceremonies were not free of cruelty. The Ainu, for example, goaded their sacrificial bear with arrows before strangling it. The

Tragically, it is this negative image of the grizzly that has largely prevailed in the last few centuries Under its persuasion, grizzlies have been knifed, harpooned, trapped and poisoned. They have been lassoed by teams of horsemen and literally pulled apart; they have been set upon by dogs. Above all, they have been shot by the thousands or, more likely, hundreds of thousands. As British philosopher Thomas Carlyle once observed, the "genuine use" of gunpowder is to make "all men alike tall"; and high-powered guns have more than levelled the disparities between ourselves and bears. But rifles have not been our only weaponry. Bulldozers, chain saws, plows and paving machines have all supported the attack.

Grizzly bears, clearly creatures with exceptional power to move the human mind, have been pushed slowly but relentlessly into a severe population decline. Two or three centuries ago, for example, there were about fifty thousand grizzlies in the contiguous United States; today there are fewer than nine hundred, occupying 1 per cent of their former range. During the last century, the species has been exterminated in ten states and is now listed as "threatened" in the contiguous states.

In western Europe, the situation is far worse. In Norway, where there may have been about 2000 bears in the year 1600, there are perhaps 50. Finland and Sweden may have a combined population of 300 to 500. In Italy—miraculously—there are about 100, mostly in Abruzzi National Park in the Apennines near Rome. About 150 remain in Spain; in France, no more than 20. The French population has stopped breeding and could be lost within ten or fifteen years. Already people speak of the survivors as "walking dead."

In eastern Europe—especially the Carpathian and Balkan mountains, Yugoslavia and Albania— there are still thought to be several thousand bears. But in the Middle East and along the southern fringe of the species' range in Asia, extinction seems imminent. In Japan, the holy bears of the Ainu are now suffering what one biologist calls "horrendous persecution" in the interests of agriculture, forestry and sport hunting.

All told, there are probably about 180,000 grizzlies in the world today. By far the majority—about 100,000—live in the Soviet Union. Sizable populations also inhabit Alaska (perhaps 40,000) and western Canada, mostly Yukon and British Columbia (another 20,000 or so). But as a Soviet biologist has recently pointed out, even relatively large numbers offer "no basis for an attitude of calm." Alaskan researchers echo this anxiety: ". . . grizzlies are still abundant [in this state], fishing the same streams and traveling the same age-old trails as their ancestors did thousands of years ago. But many of the. . . pressures that led to the species' disappearance elsewhere are becoming evident in Alaska."

Around the hemisphere, those pressures are the same: loss of habitat and excessive shooting.

If we permit this process to continue, it will surely be a sign that we have lost our way. Guided by streetlights rather than starlight, we risk losing our connections with the forces that sustain and renew life on our planet. "The reason grizzlies are not extinct is that they have power," George Blondin says. Perhaps they will now have the power to help us change our way of life.

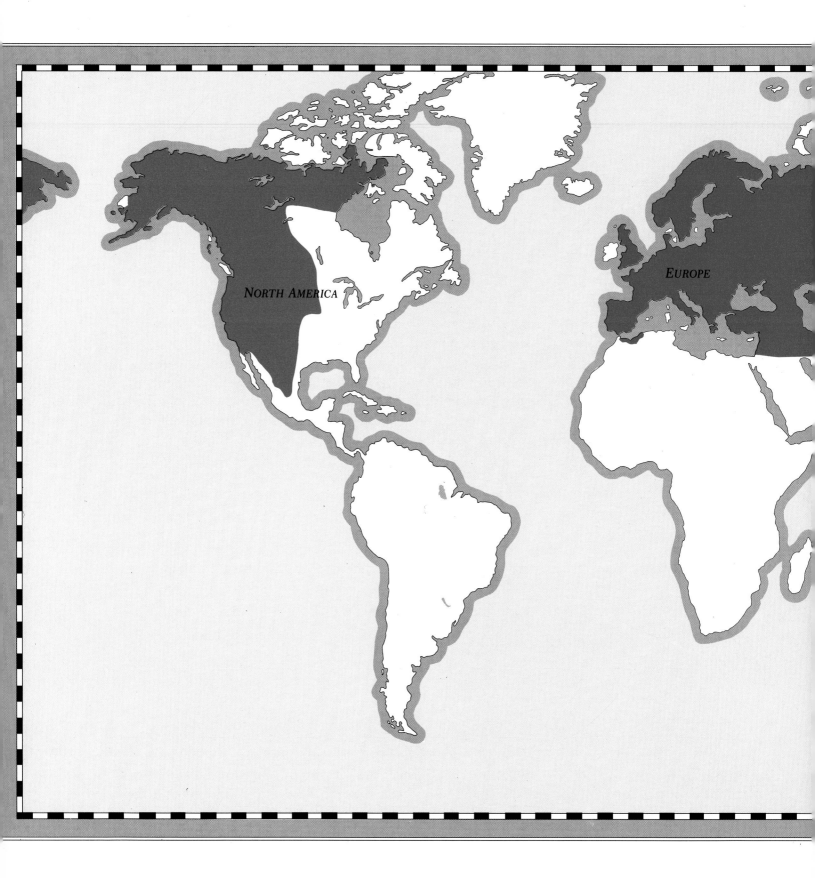

NORTH AMERICA

EUROPE

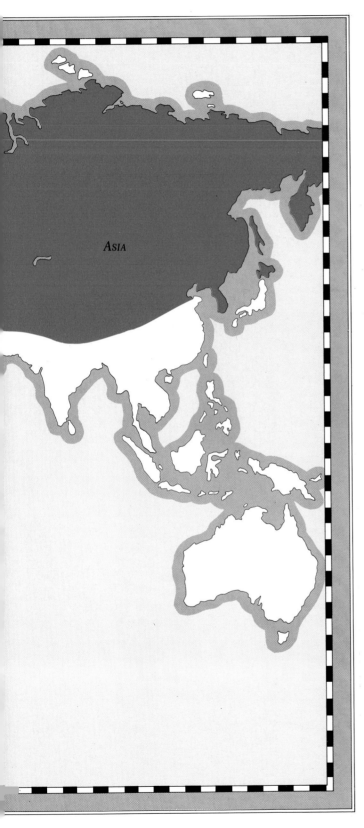

ASIA

HISTORIC DISTRIBUTION OF THE GRIZZLY
BEAR, *URSUS ARCTOS*

Based on information provided by Peter Clarkson, N.W.T. Renewable Resources, and
Stephen Herrero, *Bear Attacks: Their Causes and Avoidance.*

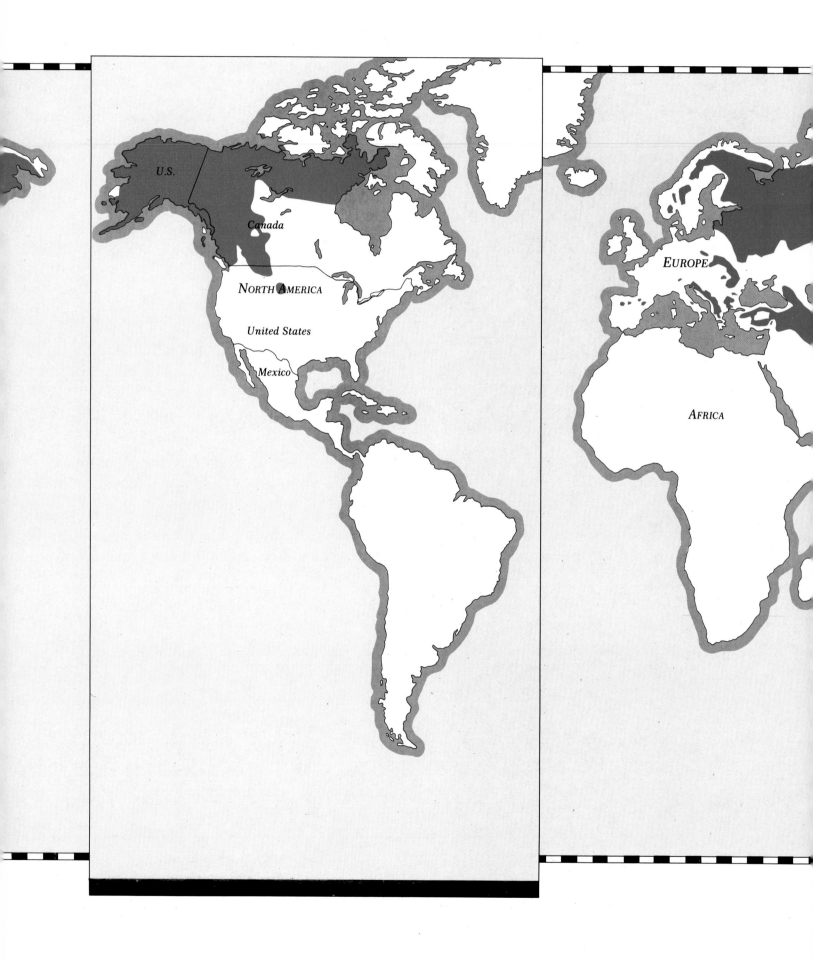

U.S.

Canada

NORTH AMERICA

United States

Mexico

EUROPE

AFRICA

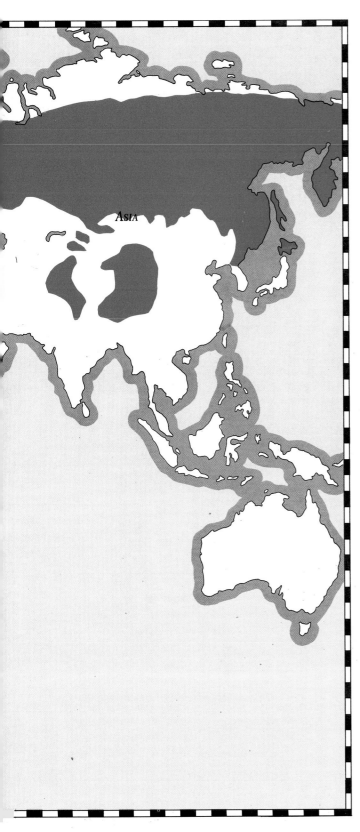

PRESENT DISTRIBUTION OF THE GRIZZLY
BEAR, *URSUS ARCTOS*

Based on information provided by Chris Servheen, U.S. Grizzly Bear Recovery
Coordinator, and Stephen Herrero, *Bear Attacks: Their Causes and Avoidance.*

The grizzly is known to science simply and emphatically as "the bear," Ursus arctos. Ursus and arctos mean "bear" in Latin and Greek, respectively. In fact as in name, the grizzly is the most bearish of living animals. It embodies the essence of bearness and the wild, free beauty of the country that it roams. Here grizzlies fish for salmon amid a flurry of scavenging gulls. KARL SOMMERER

A family of grizzlies enjoys the fresh, green solitude of a mountain pass. A resident of Europe, Asia and North America, Ursus arctos—*also known as the grizzly, brown, big brown, Alaska brown, red and horse bear—is the most widely distributed species of bear in the world.* KARL SOMMERER

Although there are subtle differences in appearance between grizzlies from various parts of the world, members of the species can always be recognized by their massive build, muscled shoulder humps, broad, flat faces and long claws. Coat colour is not much help in identifying them, since individuals may vary from honey-blond to red to black. ALLAN AND SANDY CAREY

I had never seen a grizzly and we did not see one on our 20-mile hike, although it was superb bear country. One lone track in a patch of mud is all we saw. In innocent wonder I gazed at the imprint. It was a symbol, more poetic than seeing the bear himself—a delicate and profound approach to the spirit of the Alaska wilderness.

—ADOLPH MURIE, *The Grizzlies of Mount McKinley*

An ambling grizzly has pressed its tracks into fresh mud. Unlike most animals, which run on their toes, bears walk flat-footed, as we do ourselves. The Crees sometimes called them four-legged humans, partly because of this similarity. Grizzly tracks are wider than a hiking boot and are disconcertingly deep and long clawed.

To distinguish grizzly tracks from those of the smaller and less dangerous American black bear, check for evidence of long front nails. Joined toe marks are also a common characteristic of grizzly tracks. TOM WALKER

The water churns as two grizzlies square off in a dispute over fishing rights. TIM FITZHARRIS

Anyone for a hot guitar lick? Actually, this bear is just indulging in a scratch. In Europe, the grizzly is now most familiar as a tractable and good-humoured zoo animal. TOM AND PAT LEESON

◄ *Over the millennia, grizzlies have appeared in human cultures in many different forms, not all of them profound. In our time, for example, they have provided the inspiration for Smokey the Bear, the cartoon character who instructs us on the dangers of forest fires. (Ironically, forest fires are generally beneficial to grizzly bears because they maintain the open habitat that the bears require.)*

Although these two may look like they are waiting in line for their ranger hats, they are actually standing up to get a better look at something that has aroused their curiosity. TOM WALKER

Carefree in the summer sun, this grizzly seems to be having a chat with its toes. Perhaps it was natural antics like this that inspired circus owners to train grizzlies as acrobats and clowns. Some trainers rank grizzlies higher than horses or dogs in intelligence. ERWIN AND PEGGY BAUER

Picnic time for teddy bears? Real-life "teddies" love to play, especially with their siblings. No one is likely to be hurt in a friendly tussle like this. LEN RUE JR./LEONARD RUE ENTERPRISES

▶ *One of the strongest and most surprising aspects of the bear's presence in modern culture is the teddy bear, obviously inspired by young charmers like the one seen here. With its round baby face and clumsy, toddlerlike ways, a bear cub tugs at the human heartstrings. The teddy was created in 1902, and as much as the computer or space station, it stands as an emblem of the twentieth century.* LEONARD LEE RUE III

Female grizzlies continue to nurse their young as long as the family stays intact. To some peoples, they have seemed to embody the mysterious power of the Earth to create and nurture life—and to destroy it. Female grizzlies will sometimes attack other bears and, very occasionally, humans, if they decide that their young are at risk. ERWIN AND PEGGY BAUER

◄ An aspect of grizzly behaviour that has made a deep impression on humankind is the devoted care that the females give to their young. The Greek deity Artemis was a bear goddess, and so was Dea Artio, a Celtic deity who was formerly honoured at Bern, Switzerland, literally the city of the bear. An ancient bronze statue of this goddess was unearthed in Bern in 1832.

A feminine principle of birth, growth, decay, and rebirth lies at the heart of the veneration of the bear, for the bear is the supreme model —and therefore the guiding spirit—of the theme of renewal.

—PAUL SHEPARD AND BARRY SANDERS,

The Sacred Paw

Young bears remain under their mother's protection for about two and a half years, sometimes longer. These twins, at right, are nearly as big as their dam.
ART WOLFE

Haloed by flying droplets, a bear shakes dry with casual strength. FRED BRUEMMER

Although other animals have been honoured by humankind, none has enjoyed such widespread and intense devotion as the bear. In some northern cultures, celebrations were held whenever a grizzly was killed, to atone for its death. Often the dead animal was identified as the mate or son of the Bear Mother, a woman who, in myth, was married to a bear. It was through this union that the people learned how to honour the slain bear and thereby ensure that its spirit would be reborn. JOHNNY JOHNSON/VALAN PHOTOS

The illustrious is coming
Pride and beauty of the forest
'Tis the master come among us,
Covered with his friendly fur-robe,
Welcome, loved one from the glenwood.

—FINNISH BEAR-FESTIVAL SONG

Grizzlies are superhuman in both size and strength. Although most fights end without fatalities, many adults, especially males, carry the scars of past disputes.

Through the centuries, kings and warriors have sometimes claimed to be descended from bears and have sought to emulate the ferocity of their supposed "forebears." Britain's legendary King Arthur, for example, took his name from the root for "bear." Sadly, his heraldic animal has been extinct in Britain for the last thousand years. ERWIN AND PEGGY BAUER

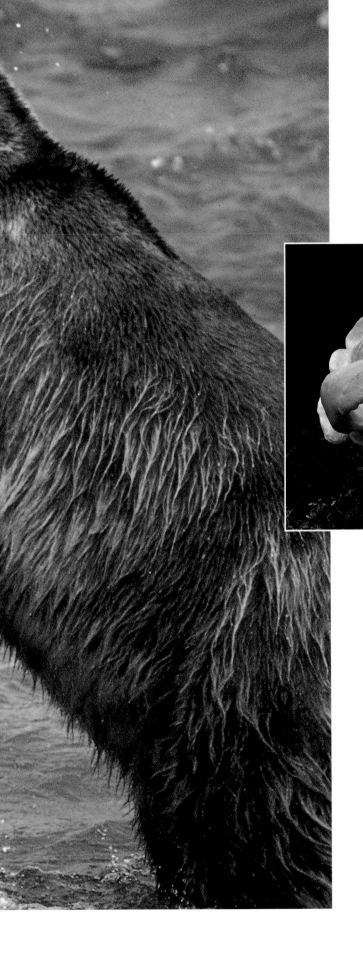

In some cultures, grizzly skulls were placed in trees to protect and honour them; in others, the whole skeleton was buried with care and ceremony. In northern Sweden, for example, such graves have been discovered and excavated in recent decades. ERWIN AND PEGGY BAUER

Western Europe is still home to a small number of grizzlies. This old male, striding through late spring snow in northern Finland, is one of the few hundred that remain in that country. Because of excessive hunting, the population is thought to depend on a continual natural influx of bears from the U.S.S.R. HANNU HAUTALA

▶ ▶ In western Europe, human pressure has altered the nature of the grizzly bear. Since bold, aggressive animals are most likely to run afoul of humankind, they have been selectively removed over the centuries. Conversely, shy, fearful bears have had a better chance to survive and breed. The result is a race of timid, self-effacing bears who are seldom seen. This photograph gives us a rare look at one of the last surviving grizzlies in the Italian Alps. FABIO OSTI

Determined to protect a carcass it has been eating, a bear in northern Finland shoves a boulder on top for extra security. ANTTI LEINONEN

Perhaps we won't lose the grizzly altogether. Perhaps we'll just change it into something else. Take a remnant population, especially a small inbreeding one. Keep blowing away the big, the bold, the conspicuous. And out of the shallow gene pool "climbs a scaled-down version, meek and mild. A grizzly in name only. . . . "

—DOUGLAS H. CHADWICK, quoting Chris Servheen,"'Grizz:' Of Men and The Great Bear,"
National Geographic

Although this bear has come into the open for a look around, the bears of Europe generally keep to the cover of forests and may only be active by night.
LEONARD LEE RUE III

In North America, grizzlies are now found only in the mountains and northern wilderness. Unlike their European cousins, they spend much of their time in open country—meadows, tundra, avalanche chutes and the like. Until quite recently, they also roamed across the Great Plains, where they were part of the now-vanished world of the buffalo. TOM AND PAT LEESON

[When] you leave y^e woods behind
. . . you have beast of severall kind
The one is a black a Buffillo great

Another is an outgrown Bear wch is good meat

His skin to gett I have used all y^e ways I can
He is mans food & he makes food of man
His hyde they would not me it preserve
But said it was a god and they should starve

—HENRY KELSEY, 1690, near La Pas, Manitoba.
Kelsey was one of the first Europeans to see a grizzly in
North America. He shot it.

Although they often leave the forest to feed, North American grizzlies return to the trees for rest and safety. Here, at the forest edge, a family stands on the alert. If the mother detects danger, she and the cubs will likely flee into the shrubbery.
TOM WALKER

A grizzly emerges from its resting place in the underbrush. Biologists fear that advancing human development will threaten the survival of the grizzly, even where it occurs in good numbers today. JOHNNY JOHNSON

Natural explorers and opportunists, the great bears are able to exploit an astonishing range of habitats across three continents. Here a female and a young cub take on the challenge of a salmon stream. JOHNNY JOHNSON

◀ *Without even bothering to get out of the water, this grizzly sinks his teeth into the flesh of a sockeye. The biggest, fattest, most successful populations of bears live where there is a rich source of protein, such as salmon or trout. But even these bears may be endangered by human pressures. In Alaska, for example, the human population has increased eightfold in the last fifty years, with a corresponding expansion of industry and hunting. Biologists are concerned about what will happen in the next half century.* MARTIN W. GROSNICK

Where concentrated sources of protein are not available, grizzlies subsist on plants and on humbler meats, such as the ants and grubs found under rocks. Bears that live in less productive habitats are particularly susceptible to the ill effects of overhunting and loss of habitat. PAT AND TOM LEESON

There seems to be a tacit assumption that if grizzlies survive in Canada and Alaska, that is good enough. It is not good enough for me. . . . Relegating grizzlies to Alaska is about like relegating happiness to heaven; one may never get there.

—ALDO LEOPOLD, *A Sand County Almanac*

A mother and cubs stroll across a tidal flat in Alaska.
ERWIN AND PEGGY BAUER

A bear pauses for a drink in prime grizzly habitat. KARL SOMMERER

For the last several centuries, the grizzly has been persecuted as a bloodthirsty monster and a common pest. The future of the species depends in large part on our ability to perceive it with greater honesty.
ART WOLFE

RICK MCINTYRE

NATURAL HISTORY

rizzlies are among the most awesome of living animals. An exceptionally large male may weigh 600 kilograms (1300 pounds), or more than six huge men, yet it could outrun the fastest man on Earth. Its strength is immense. With the swat of a heavy paw, it smashes the spine of a moose. With one crunch of its massive jaws, it shatters the thigh bone of a caribou. In a fight with another bear, it can grab its opponent in its teeth and throw it to the ground.

Yet for all its heroic proportions, the grizzly is vulnerable. Around the world over the last thousand years, its domain has shrunk by half. Although we cannot precisely plot its numerical decline, we know that the population loss has been both gradual and drastic and that it continues largely unchecked.

The forces that have been deployed against the grizzly—industrial civilization and firearms—have affected other creatures as well, yet not all species have suffered equally. One thinks, for example, of the North American coyote, which has been trapped, shot, poisoned and dynamited for decades, and which still exists in large numbers over an extensive range; or of the wolf, which is sometimes able to quickly rebound from attempts at "control." What is it that makes the grizzly so susceptible to harm?

The answer to this question lies in the nature of the grizzly and the way it has evolved. Evolution, like politics, is the art of the possible; it is always constrained by the genetic materials at hand. To put it another way, no species is able to choose its ancestors. Grizzly bears trace their inheritance back about 25 million years, to a group of small carnivores called the miacids, which also eventually gave rise to weasels, cats and dogs. (Members of the dog family—foxes, wolves, coyotes and "man's best friend"—are the bears' closest living relatives.) The miacids lived in trees, and for many millions of years, bears kept faith with this arboreal ancestry. Of the eight modern species of bears, six still live in the forests and readily climb trees; they are the sun, sloth and spectacled bears of the tropics, the panda, and the American and Asian black bears.

Then began the long, slow turmoil of the Ice Age. It was during this period, in northern Asia, that the grizzly arose. (The eighth species, the polar bear, appeared as the glaciers receded and is a descendant of the grizzly.) Still capable of occupying treed areas, the grizzly was specially adapted to occupy the vast, treeless landscapes that were exposed by the glaciers. Then, as now, it was characteristically a creature of the edge lands, where forest meets open terrain. Among the foods available in its expanded habitat were plant roots and ground squirrels, which had to be dug from the earth. The grizzly was built for this labour, with stout claws (less deeply curved than those of climbing bears) and massive muscles across the shoulders and back.

In return for these advantages, the grizzly paid a price: the partial loss of its ancestral agility in trees. Grizzlies, even large adults, can and do climb, sometimes clambering four or five metres (about fifteen feet) above ground, a statistic worth noting in case you ever have to seek refuge from an attack! They are, however, less adroit and less inclined to seek the treetops than other species, such as black bears. As grizzlies became less arboreal, they became more fierce. Grizzly expert Stephen Herrero reinforces these observations with an anecdote:

> A young national park naturalist, fresh from training, was lecturing to a crowd of tourists, discussing the differences between black bears and grizzly bears. The naturalist said that a good way to tell the species of a given bear was to sneak up on the bear in question and kick it in the rump, then to immediately run and climb a tree. If the bear climbs up the tree after you it is a black bear.

> An old-timer in the audience thought this test too elaborate. He said all you have to do to discover the species' identity is to sneak up on the bear, kick it in the rump, wait a split-second, and then if you are still alive the bear was a black.

The usual response of a grizzly to a human being is fear or, at most, curiosity. From his extensive research, Herrero has concluded that "most interactions with grizzly bears do not lead to injury. Most don't even involve aggression." A typical bear-attack story ends before it has really begun; either the bear (tipped off by its sensitive nose) avoids the encounter altogether, or else it investigates, then turns and runs.

With these facts in mind, there is still no doubt that grizzlies are markedly more aggressive and more dangerous to people than most other species of bears. Mountain man and writer Andy Russell, who has spent his whole long life in the bear country of Alberta, attests to this fact with characteristic wit. Comparing the grizzly with the American black bear, he says, is "like standing a case of dynamite beside a sack of goose feathers."

The grizzly's comparative ferocity is probably an adaptation to life in open country. When a family of black bears feels threatened, the cubs protect themselves by scooting up the nearest tall tree; the mother either climbs up behind them or stands her ground and defends them with great show but little follow-through. These traits have served black bears, and their ancestors, for millions of years. But during the Ice Age, when those ancestral bears moved onto the barrenlands—not a tree in sight—the old behaviours no longer worked. Under the new conditions, the best way to protect cubs was to avoid trouble or, failing that, to stand and fight. If a mother bear was meek, she would likely lose her family, perhaps to a saber-toothed tiger or some other predator. But if she was fierce, she was more likely to bring her young successfully through to adulthood and pass her fighting spirit on to future generations. To this day, a female grizzly with cubs is among the most aggressive of bears and the kind you want least to come upon by surprise.

Since the extinction of the Ice Age predators, grizzlies have had no enemies except people—and one another. The greatest natural danger to young bears (a threat against which mother grizzlies are constantly on the alert) is posed by adult male bears. Males play no part in rearing cubs. Instead, they spend their time feeding, resting, visiting females in season and often travelling. The area used by an adult male can be vast, usually between 300 and 1000 square kilometres (between about 100 and 400 square miles), depending on the local food supply. The smallest home ranges are found where nature's larder is abundantly stocked; on Kodiak Island in the gulf of Alaska, for example, bears feast at rich salmon streams, and a male can do well on a range of less than 50 square kilometres (20 square miles). By contrast, in the more austere habitats of the Alaskan interior, one male on record roamed an area of 5700 square kilometres (2200 square miles). That is roughly equivalent to two thousand sections of farmland or to the entire Canadian province of Prince Edward Island.

As they rove these large domains, adult males may go for weeks without meeting other bears; yet it may not be entirely accurate to describe them as solitary. Instead, they are likely part of a sparse and unsociable community, with a tenuous social order quite unlike our own. Male bears share parts of their living space with other males (which is to say that their home ranges overlap). What's more, each male's terrain encloses the domains of several female bears, which are much smaller than those of the males— perhaps 100 to 400 square kilometres (40 to 150 square miles). Yet neighbouring bears seldom visit the same area at the same time. How do they manage to stay out of each other's way?

One possibility is that they keep track of one another's movements by checking rub-mark trees. These are, in the beginning, ordinary trees, which through convenience and tradition come to serve the local bears as communal rubbing posts. Often they are located along streams or in other places where the lay-of-the-land channels travel along a narrow pathway. Veteran grizzly watcher Adolph

Murie told of exploring a stream course in Denali National Park:

> The [bear] traffic was so heavy that not only were the individual bear steps deeply worn, but much-used bear trees were closely spaced. I believe that the power of suggestion has given all bear travelers numerous itches, with the result that itching and rubbing on trees has increased through the years. . . .
>
> In a thorough scratching, the back, sides, rear, stomach, head, and neck are all massaged. Occasionally, the maneuvers suggest the latest "twist" dance. . . . One bear standing on hind legs against a pole, raised and lowered herself, wriggling her body as part of the down movement to add to the effect.

As Murie notes, curious "mark trails," consisting of distinct, deeply worn footprints, may add interest to the site, and the trees themselves are unmistakable: scraped, worn, battered and coated with bear hair. To a grizzly, they must have an olfactory presence as well, offering an intriguing mixture of highly personal smells for the information of the next itchy traveller who happens along.

The bears' sense of smell is almost unparalleled, far better than any dog's, much less our own. The area of mucous membrane with which they detect scents is one hundred times larger than that in the human nose. Bears also have the biggest brains relative to body size of any carnivore, giving them ample capacity to interpret and remember what they smell. Researchers speculate that they may even navigate over long distances by following faint scents carried by prevailing winds. When a young "problem" grizzly in Alaska was airlifted to a new area, it soon found its way home, a journey of more than 270 kilometres (170 miles) over unfamiliar terrain. Others have made similar returns over somewhat lesser distances. Either grizzlies have a sixth sense—perhaps magnetic—or else they literally follow their nose.

For a bear, out of sight does not mean out of mind, and it is conceivable that grizzlies keep track of their far-flung neighbours by smell. There seems little doubt that males rely on scent to find potential mates. If a female grizzly lives to extreme old age—about twenty-five years—she may only come into breeding condition half a dozen times. Many females do not breed until they are four or five years old, or even older; after that, they come into heat, on average, every three or four years, each time for a period of a few weeks. (This low rate of reproduction is typical for an animal with few natural enemies.) Being on the spot to take advantage of these brief and sporadic opportunities is a major preoccupation of male grizzlies.

Days before a female is fully ready to breed, an eager suitor trundles into view, drawn by her alluring scent. At first the female may be wary. At any other time in her life, a male bear signals DANGER to her and especially to her offspring. Male grizzlies kill cubs (somehow, presumably, managing to spare their own progeny). As many as two thirds of cubs die in their first year, and although there is a possibility that some are lost to starvation or disease, marauding males are the only proven cause of death. This behaviour is not as perverse as it may seen, since females that lose their cubs advance rapidly into their next estrus and may provide the male with an extra chance to breed. In the game of evolution, the one who dies with the most offspring wins.

Grizzlies mate in spring and summer, sometime between May and July, but the females do not become pregnant immediately. In adapting to the feast-and-famine cycle of the Northern Hemisphere, bears have developed a procedure called delayed implantation, which simply means that the fertilized egg floats in the female's womb for several months. If the female fails to get enough to eat during the summer, the egg will die. But if she is well fed, it will settle into the uterine wall and develop while she is hibernating. In either case, the female has her summer free for serious eating, without the encumbrance of a pregnancy.

The cubs are born in midwinter, in litters of one to four. The number depends in part on the local food supply, but twins are probably most common overall. At birth, grizzlies are helpless and so small that a newborn would easily fit into your cupped hands. But they grow fast, nourished by their mother's rich milk, and are robust and playful by the time warm weather arrives.

Stephen Herrero once had the fun of watching a trio of spring cubs make their first forays outdoors in Banff National Park. It was mid-April, and the slope above the den was still covered with snow. One of the cubs' favourite sports was to charge up the hill, then let themselves go and toboggan towards the den. One after another they landed with a thump—right on their mother's head. She was lying, lethargic, in the mouth of the den. With scarcely a flicker of reaction, she permitted the cubs to fall off her back and do it all over again. Herrero explains that she had not yet completed the physiological transition out of dormancy (but maybe, like many single parents, she was just too tired to care!).

Bear cubs are atwitch with curiosity, a characteristic they will retain in large measure throughout their lives. Every crook and cranny, every pebble and stick must be studied, sniffed, tasted and pawed. The focus of the youngsters' attention is their mother, for by watching and imitating her, they will learn the business of being a bear.

The main subject of the cubs' apprenticeship is learning what to eat. Bears are omnivores, which means that they choose both plant and animal foods in season: stems, leaves, bark, roots, nuts, seeds, flowers, fruits, ants, grubs, birds' eggs, rustlings, rodents, crustaceans, fish, garbage, camp foods, carrion and fresh meat. It does not mean that they can eat anything and everything. At high latitudes, grizzlies are only active and able to feed for five months of the year; farther south, they may be allotted two months more. Everywhere they face a deadline; their eating is urgent. Each mouthful must make the maximum possible contribution towards the year's requirements.

Grizzlies are also constrained by their anatomy. As members of the order Carnivora, they have inherited the meat eaters' unspecialized, tubelike gut. Flesh is easy to digest, but plants—which form most of the grizzly's diet—are more challenging. Animals such as rabbits and deer, which have evolved as herbivores, have multichambered stomachs or other adaptations for breaking down cellulose. Lacking these features, bears cannot digest their food with top efficiency.

Grizzlies must find digestible, high-quality food and consume it in large quantitites. By following their mothers, young bears learn which plants are most worthwhile and where these can be found;

bears are not born knowing these things. The best places to forage change from week to week. Fresh greens, for example, are an important grizzly food because young, growing plants are low in cellulose and high in protein. Look for them in early spring on south-facing hillsides; then, as green-up spreads across the valley, check the north side. Later in the season, move upslope, following spring to higher elevations; or visit moist meadows and stream beds where the plants stay succulent.

Be in the right place at the right time. Tender roots can be found on eastern slopes when those elsewhere have gone tough. Moose or caribou calves can be captured in their birthing habitat for a few weeks. Salmon and trout can be caught as they crowd upstream to spawn—but in which rivers? at what time? Learn where to find the biggest berry patches; learn what to eat if the berries fail.

Eat. Play, rest, keep out of harm's way. Eat.

And so the seasons pass. By late fall, the cubs are little butterballs, about six times heavier than when they first tumbled out of the den. Their mother too is gaining fast, perhaps as much as a kilogram a day. Adult females weigh less than adult males (100 to 200 kilograms, or 200 to 400 pounds, on average, as opposed to 200 to 300 kilograms, or 400 to 700 pounds, for males.) But females often experience larger seasonal weight gains. By the time she enters hibernation, the mother bear is rippling with fat and may be nearly double her spring weight.

Nobody knows how grizzlies tell that it is time to den. Perhaps it is some association of external signals—day length, snowfalls, shortage of food—and internal readiness. The body says: bedtime. By late fall, the bears have prepared their dens. Often these are simple burrows dug into hillsides, sometimes lined with grass, twigs, leaves and moss; the chamber is just large enough to accommodate the individual or the family that will occupy it. (Cubs generally hibernate with their mothers until they are two years old; they may then den with each other for another one to three years.) Somehow grizzlies often select places where the snow will later settle in thick, insulating drifts, a skill that seems to develop with experience.

Inside, a good den is quiet, snug and warm. The bear rolls up into a ball, with its nose nestled into its paws. Its body temperature drops by a few degrees and its heartbeat slows. Does it dream of green grass?

Grizzlies are vulnerable because they are what they are. Like all other creatures, they must live within the limits of their own unique evolutionary success. Their achievements have been considerable. Forest dwellers, they have acquired the ability to inhabit open terrain. Meat eaters, they have made the transition to a diet that consists largely of plants. They have even become able to live for half of the year without food. But in the process, they have become potentially aggressive, a characteristic that brings them into direct conflict with humankind. Their unrelenting hunger draws them towards garbage dumps, ranches and farms, and their need for large expanses of habitat is at odds with our own demand for space. They reproduce so slowly that once their population begins to decline, it cannot quickly rebound. This is simply the nature of the bear, a complex reality to which we must learn to adapt.

The white V *on the chest of this eager young cub will disappear as it grows to maturity.* ALAN AND SANDY CAREY

Grizzly bear courtship is a nervous affair. The female, in particular, seems to vacillate between interest and fear. She may dart away for short distances or charge at the male until he backs away. The male, for his part, may try to confine the female within a restricted space. But over the days or weeks that the pair is together, they do have moments of peaceful intimacy when they lick and nuzzle one another gently. They may also sleep together, side by side or nose touching nose. ERWIN AND PEGGY BAUER

Grizzlies usually mate sometime between May and July. Males are thought to find females by smell, relying on olfactory clues like those left on rubbing posts. They often travel eagerly at this time of year, sniffing the ground and the breeze for the scent of a potential mate. Sometimes they get so engrossed in their search that they neglect to eat for hours at a stretch. TOM WALKER

As they become more comfortable together, courting grizzlies sometimes play. But once their mating is complete, no trace of this easy relationship remains. The animals separate without a backward glance and may go on to choose other mates. Both male and female grizzlies are promiscuous. TOM WALKER

If a second male grizzly intrudes on a courting pair, the smaller of the suitors may take the hint and run. Otherwise, there is likely to be a noisy brawl—snarling, growling, flying spittle, bloody injuries—which leaves the loser firmly in retreat. For her part, the female may take action against intruders of her own sex. But sometimes grizzlies overcome their intolerance and settle briefly into a cozy ménage à trois, *either two males with one female or, as shown here, a male with two sows.*
AUBREY LANG/VALAN PHOTOS

Mating grizzlies may remain coupled for the better part of an hour (at no little cost, it seems, to the female's ears!). TOM WALKER

Bears couple in the middle of winter, and not after the fashion of other quadrupeds; for both animals lie down and embrace each other. The female then retires by herself to a separate den, and there brings forth on the thirtieth day, mostly five young ones. When first born, they are shapeless masses of white flesh, a little larger than mice; their claws alone being prominent. The mother then licks them gradually into proper shape. . . .

—PLINY, *Natural History*

At birth, the grizzly is blind and toothless and weighs about 500 grams. Although mating occurs in spring or summer, the embryos do not begin to develop for several months. The young are born in midwinter, in litters of one to four, in the secret darkness of the hibernation den. Few people have ever seen a pregnant grizzly or a newborn cub, though that hasn't prevented speculation about the process over the centuries. **LEONARD LEE RUE III**

Warmed by the bright sun of springtime in Yugoslavia, three young cubs snuggle inside the hollow tree where their mother hibernated and gave birth to them. ALOJZIJE FRKOVIC

Adult males are the first to leave their hibernation dens, emerging in advance of spring when the weather is still blustery and food must be sought. Lone females and those with older cubs follow as the season moderates, but females with new cubs stay snug inside their dens for another month or two, until spring has fully arrived. RICK MCINTYRE

Young cubs do their best to stay close by mother's side. If a spring cub accidentally gets lost, it may cry and bawl in a loud, harsh voice until its mother comes to its aid. Most female grizzlies are attentive parents, who tend and "discipline" their offspring and are willing, if necessary, to defend them to the death. Even so, two thirds or more of the cubs may die within their first year. The grizzly's rate of reproduction is painfully slow. JOHNNY JOHNSON

[Every few hours the female] would leave off whatever she was doing and half rear and spin on her heels to go over backward on the ground. She would hardly be flattened out before the cub would land ecstatically on the vast expanse of hairy bosom and grab a tit while... [the mother] caressed it with gentle muzzle and paws. The cub would move from one dug to another until all were sucked dry; and then they would play a while, with the young one galloping and bucking up and down her belly, smelling noses, and playfully swatting with paws.

—ANDY RUSSELL, *Grizzly Country*

Grizzlies nurse their cubs for a few minutes every two or three hours, either sitting upright like this or lying flat on the ground. KARL SOMMERER

Having found an interesting twig to chew, this young grizzly settles down to rest. RICK MCINTYRE

When there are two or three cubs in a family, they spend hours of each day wrestling and chasing each other. But when there's only one youngster, Mother is called upon to serve as principal playmate. ESTHER SCHMIDT/VALAN PHOTOS

Huddled together for security, twin cubs wait for their mother to return from fishing. JOHNNY JOHNSON

This bear was killed and partly eaten by another grizzly. Such incidents are rare and usually occur when females try to defend their young against large males. ALOJZIJE FRKOVIC

As their mother snaps to full alert, three large cubs doze in a companionable heap. During the spring of their third or fourth year, these youngsters will give up their mother's protection. If they fail to leave on their own, their mother will chase them away as she prepares to breed again. After separating from their mother, the adolescents may stay together for a year or more. AUBREY LANG/VALAN PHOTOS

. . . three females, each with three cubs came together and changed [cubs] . . . almost daily. There were times, however, when a group remained together for as long as two days. When cub interchange was first observed, females appeared to be under stress. In one instance, a female tried to stop the litter with her from leaving with another family group. She managed to keep one cub by grasping it in her mouth and tossing it down a hill. As the summer progressed . . . , the females appeared to accept litter mixing as a normal activity. . . . There was one observation of a female nursing six cubs.

—L. P. GLENN AND COLLEAGUES, "Reproductive biology of female brown bears, McNeil River, Alaska"

Except for mating season, adult grizzlies seldom seek one another's company. They may, however, be brought together by an especially rich source of food, such as a calving ground, garbage dump or spawning stream. When families associate in this way, cubs sometimes mingle, get confused and take off after the wrong female. Sometimes these foster cubs are accepted; sometimes they are killed. JEFF FOOTT

In addition to protection, a mother grizzly also unintentionally provides her youngster with a thorough tutoring in the arts of food getting. Here a cub gets a close-up view as its mother searches for fish. Sometimes bears stick their heads right under the water to look for prey, a behaviour called snorkeling. KARL SOMMERER

A cub reaches for scraps as its mother consumes a fish. Ordinarily, grizzlies do not willingly share food with one another, though a mother will tolerate a cub that stands by to snatch tidbits.

When bears congregate to fish, very large males are able to claim the best fishing holes. Females who are accompanied by large cubs, like the one shown here, rank second in the social hierarchy. Then come single adults and "teenaged" sibling groups. Females with young cubs generally stay safely on the fringes and make do with inferior places to fish. ART WOLFE

Missed! By using the standing-plunging-forepaws-mouth technique—known in common parlance as the belly flop—a bear will nab a fish every second or third try. MARTIN W. GROSNICK

◄ *This bear gives new meaning to the term* fly *fishing. Grizzlies often catch fish by watching from land and then plunging full force into the stream. Fish may be caught with the front paws alone or with the paws and mouth.* JOHNNY JOHNSON/VALAN PHOTOS

Another favourite technique is to wade into the rushing river, watch and wait, then strike with paws or mouth. Fish may be pinned to the bottom with a forepaw and picked up with the mouth or snatched straight out of the water with the teeth.
KARL SOMMERER

Dinner is served, Brooks Falls, Alaska. TOM WALKER

Too full to haul himself ashore, a successful fisherman plops down to rest beside his latest catch. Well-fed bears sometimes delicately peel the fat skin from their fish and leave the rest to be eaten by scavengers. JEFF FOOTT/VALAN PHOTOS

Only a small percentage of the world's grizzlies have access to spawning salmon or trout. In most places, the bears' taste for meat is satisfied by insects, rodents, calves and lambs, and carrion. Although grizzlies are sometimes able to kill large mammals, such as caribou and moose, they seldom bother to make the attempt. It is a sad fact that many grizzlies have been convicted and shot as cattle killers when their only "crime" was to come upon a cow after it was dead. JOHNNY JOHNSON

Andy Russell once watched as a grizzly came upon a sleeping caribou and scared it away by thumping on the ground:

This was a revealing experience. Here was a grizzly, likely weighing in the vicinity of six hundred pounds, that had spent a good half minute within ten feet of a sleeping bull caribou. He could have leaped on the animal and killed it with the same ease that a wolf would kill a rabbit, yet he had chosen deliberately to spook the caribou and let it go. More than ever I was convinced that some grizzlies never learn to kill anything bigger than a caribou calf.

—ANDY RUSSELL, *Grizzly Country*

In early spring, before green-up, bears may subsist on carrion and on roots, which they claw out of the ground with their massive front legs. A meadow in which grizzlies have been digging for roots looks as if it has been plowed. In Canada and parts of Alaska, the tubers of legumes called hedysarum or bear root are staple foods and may be sought at any time from spring to fall. RICK MCINTYRE

Since grizzlies are only able to feed for five to eight months each year, they must concentrate on obtaining large quantities of nutritious food. The early growth stages of green plants suit their purposes, being plentiful, rich in protein and easy to digest. ART WOLFE

Surrounded by spring blossoms, a grizzly nibbles on a cluster of bear flowers. The bear has given its name to a wide variety of plants, including bearberry, bear clover, bear grass, bear huckleberry, bearwood and many others. In North America alone, grizzlies probably eat more than two hundred different kinds of plants. RICK MCINTYRE

Though beautiful to our eyes, this scene holds little to interest a grizzly bear. By midsummer, when grasses reach maturity, they are high in cellulose and difficult to digest. Bears must then look elsewhere for their food. KARL SOMMERER

"The bear dreams of pears," Italian folklore suggests, and it is certainly true that grizzlies love fruit. As a rule, bears don't gain much weight early in the season, but come midsummer, when the berries get ripe, it's full steam ahead. In go the berries—as many as 200,000 in a single day—and on goes the fat. If the berry crop fails, bears may turn to roots and may be more likely to seek out human foods. RICK MCINTYRE

◀ In the fall, a grizzly's droppings may offer clear evidence of its diet. J. R. PAGE/VALAN PHOTOS

Grizzlies may go on foraging until the last possible minute before they enter their dens. Other hibernating mammals, such as ground squirrels, rouse themselves every few days to nibble a few seeds, but this bear will pass the whole winter without food or drink. Its heart will slow to eight or ten beats a minute, and its body temperature will drop by a few degrees. But should it be disturbed during hibernation, it will quickly arouse to full consciousness and may even defend itself. TERRY G. WILLIS

This frosty fisherman will soon be curled up in its den. The year-round demands of hibernation and a slow reproductive rate are among the factors that make the grizzly so vulnerable to harm. JOHNNY JOHNSON/VALAN PHOTOS

◀ *Grizzlies usually hibernate in dens that they dig themselves, often choosing places where the "roof" will be held in place by the roots of trees or shrubs. In Europe, they are also likely to use natural caves, hollow trees, brush piles and large anthills.* RICK MCINTYRE

ART WOLFE

A QUESTION OF SURVIVAL

|||| *t was a public hanging, and the media were all invited to attend. Three life-sized, plush grizzlies dangled by their necks from a bridge in Paris. Above them, a large banner revealed their dying words. "Pardon de vous avoir dérangés"* ("So sorry to have bothered you"), it read.

In the distance behind them, clearly visible, stood the Eiffel Tower, a juxtaposition that impressed one journalist. "The bear could be considered the Eiffel Tower of the Pyrénées," he said. A national monument, on the verge of ruins. The last surviving bears of France, condemned to extinction.

"The failure to create protected territories for the bear is like refusing mercy to someone on death row," said Gérard Caussimont, president of Le Groupe Ours, the lobby group that sponsored the event. For centuries, the bears of France have been trapped, poisoned and shot as agricultural pests; gradually, almost unnoticed, the population has been reduced to shreds. In the Aspe Valley of the western Pyrénées, eight or nine individuals survive; 150 kilometres (90 miles) to the east, in the Val d'Aran, there are probably another two to four. Who could doubt that this year, this week—today—it is time to act? The living space of the bears must now be preserved.

Tables are pounded; voices are raised. But there are difficulties. By their very vehemence, the bears' self-appointed defenders alarm and alienate the people whose support is most critical to their success—the villagers who live in the few valleys still occupied by bears. Like their grandparents before them, many of these mountain people are sheepherders who use the high meadows for summer pasture lands; others are involved in lumbering. They like bears, they say; they are happy to abide by the ban on hunting, which was imposed in 1958, and to accept compensation payments for livestock that is lost to predators. Several villages are even helping to establish feeding stations for the remaining bears. But activists' zealous talk about protected zones sounds suspiciously like a demand that the villagers give up lands on which they rely for their livelihood. This they do not intend to do. What do these urban yuppies expect of them? And what makes the self-righteous "greens" so sure that their solution is correct?

The controversy is urgent, intense and familiar. Hunters, loggers, tourist operators, local mayors, parks managers, forestry officials and many others have conflicting interests to assert. The ecological realities are equally disquieting: there are very few surviving bears, in a habitat that dwindles year by year. Biologists conclude that the bears have slipped beyond the point of recovery. Even with absolute protection for themselves and their living space, the bears of France could not sustain themselves.

The problem, in a nutshell, is this: small, isolated groups of animals run a very high risk of extinction. For one thing, they have no insurance against ordinary bad luck. Several seasons of poor weather or an outbreak of disease could wipe them out. Since they are isolated, there are no neighbouring animals to move in and fill the vacancies, as would normally happen. For another thing, they are susceptible to inbreeding. With few available mates, mothers breed with sons, sisters with brothers, and the genetic weaknesses of the race compound. Eventually the animals may lose their health or their fertility.

Biologists have worked out a formula that allows them to estimate the "minimum viable population" for a species. This is the smallest grouping of animals that has a high probability of surviving for the next hundred years. For grizzly bears, the total has been variously estimated at between 70 and 393 individuals. Depending on the quality of the habitat, this number of bears would require a continuous range of 5000 to 80 000 square kilometres (about 2000 to 32,000 square miles).

Three hundred and ninety-three grizzly bears in France? It is, *hélas,* far too late for that. Nonetheless, it does still seem possible—with a co-ordinated, continuous effort—to prevent the species from becoming extinct in the French Pyrénées. Achieving this goal will require a comprehensive regime of regulations and law enforcement, a regular program of bear feeding to make up for lost habitat, and occasional introductions of animals from healthy populations in other countries. The first ursine immigrants will likely be brought in from Yugoslavia and the Soviet Union within the next few years. *Glasnost* and grizzly bears.

Even at the eleventh hour something can be done, and in France as elsewhere in Europe people are building their will to begin. This is a movement of courage and hope. All the same, it is chilling to know that these animals can never be truly wild again. At best, the Pyrénées will become a kind of exotic farm, producing a carefully managed crop of grizzly bears.

Across the Atlantic, in the contiguous states, biologists still cherish the possibility of "full recovery." Six remnant populations of grizzlies survive in the Rocky Mountain states. Of these, the two with the best prospects are centred on Glacier National Park, with five hundred or six hundred bears, and around Yellowstone, where about two hundred remain. Since 1975, these animals have had the benefit of determined, detailed attention, backed by the authority of the Endangered Species Act. Mining, livestock grazing, timber cutting, beekeeping, camping, garbage disposal—a whole range of human activities has come under scrutiny. "The resources involved in this recovery effort are staggering," one biologist admits, "and the management scenario is a nightmare." Still, against all odds, the bears appear to be holding their own. What the future will hold, especially for the isolated Yellowstone population, no one can finally predict.

What has happened to the bears of western Europe and the contiguous states can happen in British Columbia, Alaska, the Caucasus, Japan or anywhere else in grizzly range. The long, slow decline towards extinction will continue unless we consciously decide to arrest it, and the same fate may also await other carnivores. "I warn you," says Monte Hummel, president of World Wildlife Fund Canada, "no dreams, no visions, no stated goals—no grizzlies, no wolves, no cougars. I'm not suggesting everyone should break down and cry when the occasional maraud-ing bear or sheep-eating wolf is killed. I'm not talking about that. . . . I'm talking about fundamental choices regarding what we want *around* on this planet fifty or a hundred years from now. . . ."

Grizzly bears need space, and the consensus is growing that large landscapes must be reserved for them if we wish to ensure that the species will survive—whole, healthy systems that still support wild populations of bears. Do it now, the experts urge, while we still have the chance. These areas won't have to be forbidden zones, where no human dare set foot. Grizzlies do not require untouched wilderness (if they did, there would be far fewer left). But they do need places where their interests are given top priority.

There are two main reasons for this need. First, most human activities reduce the quality of bear habitat. They leave the bears with less to eat and fewer places to sleep, mate and den. Logging, for example, may remove brushy cover that the bears need for resting and safety, or destroy juicy underbrush that provides important food. In some ecosystems, logging also changes the character of the woodlands. Gone are the thickets, brambles and berry bushes; in their place stand treed crop lands with an empty forest floor. No place for a grizzly bear.

Other industries, agriculture and recreation also take their toll. In range lands, livestock compete with bears by trampling wetland plants and eating spring grass. Even something as benign as a hiking trail, which scarcely alters the land, may still reduce bear habitat. Most grizzlies avoid people, and if the human intrusion goes above some mysterious threshold (which varies from bear to bear), they may stop using areas that are otherwise rich and appealing.

Fortunately, grizzlies and people are both adaptable. Faced with a loss of resources, bears may be able to compensate in other parts of their range, or they may adapt to their reduced "standard of living" by producing fewer young. Faced with the prospect of losing bears, many people—loggers, ranchers, park managers and others—have adjusted the way they do things to minimize the effect. With great care, and up to a point, humans and grizzlies can share the resources of the land.

So why the urgent need for protected areas? Added to the pressures on bear habitat is another, even more critical stress. For good reasons and bad, human beings shoot bears. The more people who use an area, the more bears are killed. "Grizzlies die of lead poisoning," says Stephen Herrero, cochairman of the International Union for the Conservation of Natural Resources/ Species Survival Commission (IUCN/SSC) Bear Specialist Group. "It's as simple as that."

One of North America's most productive populations of grizzlies lives in the Flathead Valley of southeastern British Columbia. Until a decade ago, this wild and rugged landscape remained largely untouched; then in rumbled the logging trucks. Close behind them came bear biologist Bruce McLelland, with a full kit of snares, tranquillizing darts and radio collars, to find out how the bears would respond to development. "We didn't tell timber companies how to log," he recalls. "They just did it the way they were used to." Eleven years later, to his surprise and delight, the grizzly population is in good health. "We found more bears there than anyone thought pos-

sible." In fact, McLelland thinks the bears may be poised for an upsurge.

But he is frankly worried about what the next decades will bring. The Flathead Valley is now easily accessible to anyone who cares to drive a logging road. They come in to hike, sketch, camp or fish; it seems so innocent—and then somebody bumps into a grizzly in a berry patch or slops food around his or her campsite or blunders between a mother and her cub . A hunter leaves a carcass overnight and returns to find a snarling bear on top. People get annoyed or frightened or hurt, and grizzlies end up being shot just because they're there.

And what if logging turns out to be the first step in a continuous process of development? Cabins, motels, ranches, mines—who knows what the future will bring? In other parts of British Columbia, forestry officials are suggesting that clearings created by logging should be used to pasture sheep. For grizzlies, the outcome would have the well-rehearsed inevitability of a nursery rhyme: "Bears kill people's sheep; sheep's people kill bears." In short order, the local grizzlies would be all but extinct, as they are on grazing lands elsewhere.

Several thousand kilometres farther north, Alaskan biologist John Schoen expresses similar concerns. Parts of his study area in southeastern Alaska have been logged in recent years. Here, he thinks, logging itself puts significant pressure on the bears, which stop using patches of forest that have been cut. But what concerns him far more is the number of bears that are now being killed. In one year, 20 per cent of the local population was shot, far more than ever before. The reason: new roads and an unprecedented influx of humans.

It is a rule of thumb in bear management that no more than 5 or 6 per cent of grizzlies in a given area should be killed by people each year. Most of these should be males. (After all, one male can breed with several females, and "surplus" males depress the population by killing cubs. Removing *some* of the males may actually permit the population to grow.) Stay within the guidelines, and the population will likely remain stable. Overstep them, and the bears will start to decline.

But how many grizzlies are there in the area? Five or 6 per cent of what? This no one can say with certainty. Population figures are based on guesswork—elegant, educated guesswork—but guesswork nonetheless. Grizzly research is difficult, dangerous and above all costly, with the result that few populations have been studied thoroughly. Managers must constantly extrapolate, using the little that is known to cast a dim, flickering light over vast areas of uncertainty. With the best intentions in the world, the process can go wrong, hunting limits may be set too high, and too many bears are shot. This is exactly what has happened over large areas of Alberta and British Columbia in the last decade.

This is not to say that hunters are the Bad Guys, or that no hunting should be allowed. Indeed, in several parts of the world, including France, Yugoslavia, Yukon and the Northwest Territories, groups of hunters have taken the lead in bear conservation and research. It can also be argued that a carefully controlled, legal hunt is in the long-term interest of the bears, since it gives them the economic and political status of a "resource." Still, the whole undertaking is dicey.

The risks associated with hunting are compounded by other losses. Every year grizzlies are also killed as threats to human life or property. Often the action in these sorry incidents centres on trash. Garbage, particularly food waste, is a power-packed nutritional resource that no grizzly can ignore. Eleven years after the garbage dump was closed in Yellowstone National Park, grizzlies still nose around the site, apparently hoping for one bite more. But as the Yellowstone experience proved, grizzlies that eat garbage often lose their fear of people, become dangerous and get shot.

Such losses can often be prevented through proper garbage disposal, either by using incinerators or by transporting garbage to dumps outside of bear country—all garbage, every day, with no exceptions allowed. Back-country campers have a special responsibility to hang their garbage out of reach and keep their tent sites clean.

When these precautions are taken—as increasingly they are, by individuals, parks, towns and industry—fewer grizzlies die. But given the nature of both people and bears, confrontations still arise, if not at the dump, then in the campground, the pasture, the orchard or the bee yard. Sometimes problems can be resolved by airlifting "offending" grizzlies onto more remote terrain, though bears have a frustrating tendency to come back home or get into mischief in their new locale. If the trouble is allowed to continue, female bears pass on bad habits to the next generation, and human feelings may eventually become so inflamed that they erupt in vengeance and rage. In the long run, it may be better to accept the inevitable and shoot individual grizzlies that are known to pose persistent threats.

To be realistic, we must also resign ourselves to a continuing incidence of "vandal kills." Grizzlies are shot illegally by a few mistrustful ranchers and by ignorant thrill seekers; how many animals are lost in this way is not known, though the number is thought to be significant. Grizzlies are also killed as part of the unsavory international traffic in animal parts. The statistics are macabre: 4300 bear gall bladders—365 kilograms (800 pounds)—sent from India to Japan, for use in traditional medicine, between 1981 and 1988; another 60,000 imported from China between 1979 and 1988; a recent shipment of 62 kilograms (137 pounds) that retailed for U.S.$3,968,000. Each year Japan also imports at least 600 kilograms (1300 pounds) of bear paws for its restaurants, where a bowl of bear-paw soup may sell for U.S.$850. This trade is centred on Asia and threatens not only grizzlies but also the little-known sloth, sun and Asian black bears; it also reaches into North America and elsewhere.

"The fate of many of the world's bear species will be decided in the next ten or twenty years," says Christopher Servheen, cochairman of the IUCN/SSC Bear Specialist Group. He hopes that the powers of CITES, the Convention on International Trade in Endangered Species, can be invoked to curb the bear trade before too much is lost.

There is a reasonable chance that this effort will succeed. Over the last few decades, much has been done to make parts of the world safer for grizzly bears, through law enforcement, public education and management of human activities. We have even begun, in a preliminary but practical way, to acknowledge the hard economic realities of "limits to growth." By recycling, carpooling and resisting the enticements of the latest

"necessity," we may slow our incursion into grizzly range. But the future of the grizzly bear is still not assured. The margins of error are very small, yet we are certain to go on making mistakes, both technically and politically. It is with all this in mind that people who care about bears have begun to call for grizzly reserves.

Establishing these areas would not be a miracle cure. To ensure the future of the grizzly, we must continue to do everything we know how, everywhere that it is practical, to the best of our ability. But if our best attempts go wrong (as history suggests they may), reserves would serve as a guarantee against total loss.

In British Columbia, the prime candidate for preservation is a misty coastal valley north of Prince Rupert called the Khutzeymateen. Here, in one of the last pristine watersheds on the west coast, grizzlies forage in the lush undergrowth of an ancient rain forest. Overhead, bald eagles perch on Sitka spruce that began life in the twelfth century. Four species of salmon swim up the river to spawn. "There's everything a bear could want," says biologist and preservation advocate Wayne McCrory, who has conducted research in the area.

There's also everything a logger could want, and the future of the valley is in limbo, pending the results of a government study into the potential impact of logging on the bears and their habitat. In a province where cabinet ministers sometimes speak of woodlands as "fibre farms," the outcome is not guaranteed. If the Khutzeymateen were reserved, it would become Canada's first grizzly bear sanctuary and might serve as "core habitat" for a population of bears that could be safely maintained through the centuries. Similar proposals have also been advanced elsewhere in western Canada and in Alaska, where several reserves have already been established.

These reserves would do much more than benefit grizzly bears. They would also create islands of wilderness, special places where the endless eccentric inventiveness of life could be studied, celebrated and conserved. Lichens, voles, berry bushes, salamanders, insects and snakes—all the strange and varied creations of the Earth—would be preserved on the lands set aside for bears. In a world where the rate of extinction is approaching one species a day and where ecosystems are disrupted long before they can be understood, it is essential that we safeguard portions of our remaining wilderness.

"Wilderness" is not, as the dictionary and our past practice both suggest, a synonym for "pathless waste." "Wilderness" is a verb. It is what the Earth does to create and sustain life on this planet, what it has been doing for the last 3.5 billion years, what we must hope it will continue to do for millions of years to come. In ways that are obvious, and others that are not, we need wilderness.

In an article entitled "The Ark of the Mind," Paul Shepard advances the idea that wildlife is, and always have been, essential to the growth of human consciousness. Our children, he suggests, turn to animals for their first lexicon of behaviours and attitudes (tail-wagging eagerness, purring contentment, chattering anxiety, growling ferocity). Our ancestors, for their part, looked to wildlife for insight into the fundamental mysteries of life: birth, puberty, healing, death, renewal. Today we too find ourselves moved by certain special animals, which retain the power to shape our awareness. Among these is the grizzly bear. By focussing our emotions, the grizzly permits us to understand and care about what is happening Out There and to begin to act.

"Artemis [the bear goddess] seems to beckon from the future, to call me toward who I am now to become," the Greek hero Hippolytus observed. She is also calling to us.

Grizzly populations have probably been in decline for a thousand years, but it is only in the last few decades that we have awakened to our loss. JOHNNY JOHNSON

What is man without the beasts? If all the beasts were gone, man would die from great loneliness of spirit, for whatever happens to the beasts also happens to man.

—CHIEF SEATTLE, 1855

Because grizzlies reproduce so slowly, an annual loss of about 10 per cent is the most they are able to sustain. Losses of adult females are especially damaging. Fortunately, many grizzly deaths can be avoided with reasonable care. JOHNNY JOHNSON

Historically, the main reason for the decline in grizzly populations has been excessive shooting. As a rule, the more people who move into an area, the more grizzlies end up being killed as threats to life and property, as trophies or as random targets.
JEFF FOOTT/VALAN PHOTOS

Many confrontations between people and grizzlies centre on food. Even more than humans, bears are driven to eat. Like this mother and cub (seen here hunting ground squirrels), they forage with intensity. Given the chance, they bring the same determination to obtaining human foods, such as garbage and camp supplies. Once a grizzly has tasted groceries, it is absolutely compelled to go after more, even if that means accosting hikers or breaking into camps. This behaviour usually means that the bear will be killed. TOM WALKER

Bears that learn to eat human food lose their natural fear of people and become dangerous. It is chastening to realize that one person's failure to store food or trash safely could condemn this bear to become a "problem." Proper management of garbage and food is essential, and everyone who enters grizzly range has a responsibility to help. ART WOLFE

◀ If you hike in bear country, it is essential to stay alert. Look for tracks, droppings, day beds and other signs that a bear may be around. Learn to identify important grizzly foods and seasonal habitats in the area you are visiting. The presence of a winsome young cub, like this one, should be taken as a sign that an irate mother bear may be nearby. Don't wait to encounter her; just leave quietly. TOM AND PAT LEESON

If you are travelling through dense brush or near a noisy stream, it is wise to make as much noise as you can. Bears are much more likely to be aggressive if they are surprised at close range. Incidentally, grizzlies don't rear up like this when they intend to attack. This bear just wants more information about something that interests her. KARL SOMMERER

How NOT *to behave in grizzly country! Anyone who purposely comes within fifty metres of a grizzly is courting tragedy.*
JOHNNY JOHNSON

Your best weapon to minimize the risk of a bear attack is your brain. Use it as soon as you contemplate a trip to bear country, and continue to use it throughout your stay.

—**STEPHEN HERRERO,** *Bear Attacks: Their Causes and Avoidance*

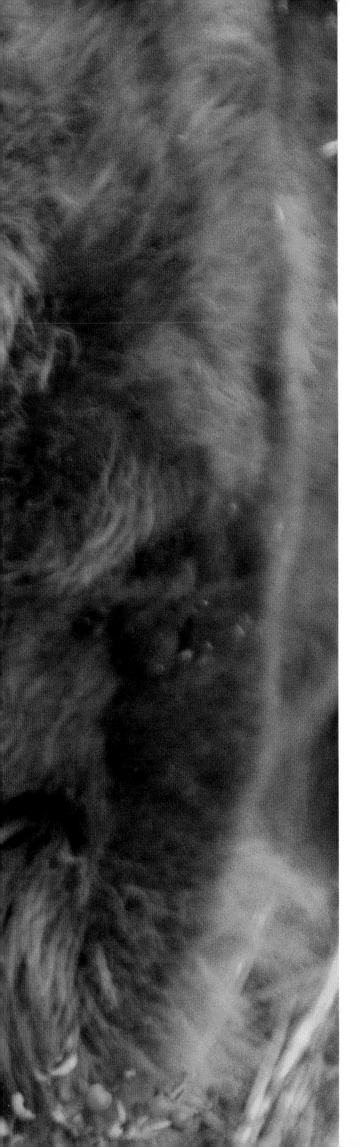

By baring its teeth, this bear leaves no doubt about its mood.

◀ *Bears do not have expressive faces, but an angry grizzly can sometimes be recognized by its lowered head, stiff posture and fixed stare. Except for garbage eaters, a grizzly that finds itself in a tight spot is likely to back away, but there is always a chance that it will charge or even attack. Grizzlies are unpredictable.*
ERWIN AND PEGGY BAUER

If you stumbled onto a grizzly bear, would you know what to do? Once a bear is alarmed, there is no surefire way to quiet it. Standing quietly or backing away is probably the safest initial response. Waving and talking are also thought to help, because they may assist the bear in recognizing you as human. ART WOLFE

A tranquillized "problem" grizzly begins its journey to a new locale. RICK MCINTYRE

◀ By learning to avoid encounters with grizzlies and to defuse confrontations that accidentally occur, we are obviously acting in our own best interests. But we are also acting in the interests of grizzly bears. Grizzlies that injure people usually end up dead or displaced onto unfamiliar terrain. Although relocation seems more merciful than death, research suggests that grizzlies do not do well after being moved. Clearly, preventing problems is the best solution.
RICK MCINTYRE

◀◀ Happily, preventive programs have been proven to work. In Alaska's Denali National Park, for example, human visitation increased eightfold (from 40,000 to 300,000 a year) during the 1970s. Predictably, the number of potentially dangerous encounters between people and bears rose from near zero to about thirty a year. In the 1980s, however, this grim pattern was broken. Although more and more people poured into the park—up to 600,000 per year—the number of bear incidents dropped sharply. No bears have been killed or moved for several years. The difference was a comprehensive plan of "people management," which was introduced in 1982. RICK MCINTYRE

All-inclusive, round-the-clock management seems to have halted the decline of grizzlies in the contiguous states. By using similar strategies, it may still prove possible to "save" small populations of grizzlies in western Europe. Here, a cub plays in a warm pool in Yellowstone National Park. ERWIN AND PEGGY BAUER

An even more heartening demonstration of the ability of grizzlies and people to coexist has taken place in the McNeil River sanctuary, some three hundred kilometres southeast of Anchorage, Alaska. McNeil River Falls has been called the best bear show on earth. People are admitted in small groups, no more than ten at a time, and their conduct is tightly supervised. Garbage and food are carefully managed, and visitors are coached to act calm and keep to the established routine of comings and goings. Although there have been a few tense moments, the only continuing problem is discouraging the occasional bear who wants to play! TOM WALKER

The bears come first at McNeil River. The Sanctuary was established to protect an unusual concentration of Alaskan brown bears. All human use is of secondary importance. We allow human activity at McNeil only to the extent that it does not significantly alter the bears' normal behavior.

—ALASKA DEPARTMENT OF FISH AND GAME

In July and August each year, thousands of salmon enter the McNeil at its mouth on Cook Inlet and hurry upstream to spawn. Soon, however, their way is blocked by a series of flat rock slabs, known as McNeil River Falls. As the fish wriggle and jump in the shallow, rushing stream, they become easy prey to bears. As many as sixty grizzlies have been known to congregate in the area at one time. KARL SOMMERER

◀ Although the bears of McNeil River Falls spar among themselves, they are not aggressive towards the people who visit them. In fact, they seem almost completely uninterested in humankind. Since the sanctuary opened in 1973, it has received about 2500 visitors, yet there has never been a human injury. JEFF FOOTT

McNeil River provides an unparalleled opportunity to study aspects of bear society, such as their spacing behaviour and social hierarchy. Researchers think that the sanctuary could be used as a model for the development of bear-viewing sites in other parts of the world. KARL SOMMERER

A grizzly is beset by a flock of squawking pirates at McNeil River Falls. KARL SOMMERER

Clearly, grizzlies are much more tolerant and adaptable than we have supposed. Grizzlies and people can coexist, but only if we are willing to try.
JEFF FOOTT

◀ *Just metres away from a line-up of clicking shutters, a McNeil River grizzly settles down for a snooze.*
KARL SOMMERER

The painstaking, one-on-one management that is practised in sanctuaries and parks cannot be extended throughout grizzly range. But the underlying attitudes will serve us everywhere. Grizzlies, as much as people, have rights—rights to peace and safety, rights to liberty. The grizzly as a species has a simple right to survive. We must value the grizzly's interests as we do our own. BETH ELDRIDGE

▶*A grizzly rests on a mat of bearberry.* TOM WALKER

The conservation movement is, at the very least, an assertion that these interactions between man and land are too important to be left to chance, even that sacred variety of chance known as economic law.

—ALDO LEOPOLD, "The Conservation Ethic," *Journal of Forestry*

A family of grizzlies hunts for ground squirrels in a wide tundra landscape. As part of the survival plan for the species, we should act now to create a network of grizzly bear reserves—wild lands and open spaces where the intricate tapestry of life has not yet been disrupted. BRIAN MILNE/FIRST LIGHT ASSOCIATED PHOTOGRAPHERS

By acknowledging the needs of grizzlies, we are also acknowledging ourselves. Human beings have a fundamental need—a spiritual, biological, economic need—for wilderness. In Our Common Future, *the Brundtland Commission recommends that every nation set aside 12 per cent of its land as ecological reserve, for our own good.* STEPHEN J. KRASEMANN/VALAN PHOTOS

Morning mist: a grizzly scatters a flock of ravens at a carcass, northern Finland. ANTTI LEINONEN

Bear Mother
mother bear
teach us to see
teach us to speak
teach us to act

JOHNNY JOHNSON

REFERENCES

If you wish to read more about grizzly bears, you couldn't do better than to start with the items marked * in this list. In addition to the literature noted below, I had the benefit of personal communication with a number of bear specialists, including those named on page vii.

Alberta Forestry, Lands and Wildlife. 1989. *Management plan for grizzly bears in Alberta.*

Alekseenko, E. A. 1968. The cult of the bear among the Ket (Yenisei Ostyaks). In *Popular beliefs and folklore tradition in Siberia*, ed. V. Dioszegi, pp. 175–91. Bloomington: Indiana University.

Ballard, W. B., et al. 1981. Causes of neonatal moose calf mortality in south central Alaska. *J. Wildl. Manage.* 45 (2): 335–42.

Barbeau, M. 1945. Bear mother. *J. of American Folklore* 59 (231): 1–12.

Bromley, M., ed. 1989. *Bear-people conflicts: proceedings of a symposium on management strategies.* Yellowknife: Northwest Terrtitories Department of Renewable Resources.

———. 1988. The status of the barren ground grizzly bear (*Ursus arctos horribilis*) in Canada. Northwest Territories Department of Renewable Resources unpublished report.

———, ed., 1985. *Safety in bear country: a reference manual.* Yellowknife: Northwest Territories Department of Renewable Resources.

Carr, H. D. 1989. *Distribution, numbers, and mortality of grizzly bears in and around Kananaskis Country, Alberta.* Alberta Forestry, Lands and Wildlife Management Branch Wildlife Research Series no. 3.

Chadwick, D. H. 1986. "Grizz": of men and the great bear. *National Geographic* 169(2): 182–213.

Clarkson, P., and I. Liepins, 1989. Inuvialuit wildlife studies, grizzly bear research, progress report, 1988–89. Wildlife Management Advisory Council (N.W.T.) Technical Report no. 8.

Cottingham, D., and R. Langshaw. 1981. *Grizzly bear and man in Canada's mountain parks.* Banff, Alta.: Summerthought.

Craighead, J. J., and J. A. Mitchell, 1982. Grizzly bear. In *Wild mammals of North America: biology management, economics*, ed. J. A. Chapman and G. A. Feldhamer, pp. 515–56. Baltimore: Johns Hopkins University Press.

Dean, F. C., et al. 1986. Observations of intraspecific killing by brown bears, *Ursus arctos*. *Canadian Field-Nat.* 100 (2): 208–11.

Dembeck, H. 1965. *Animals and men*. Garden City, N.Y.: Natural History Press.

Domico, T. 1988. *Bears of the world*. New York: Facts on File.

Dorson, R. M. 1972. *Bloodstoppers and bearwalkers*. Cambridge, Mass.: Harvard University Press.

Edsman, C.-M. 1987. Bears. In *The encyclopedia of religion*, ed. Mircea Eliade, vol. 2, pp. 86–89. New York: Macmillan.

———. 1965. The hunter, the games, and the unseen powers: Lappish and Finnish bear rites. In *Hunting and fishing: nordic symposium on life in a traditional hunting and fishing milieu in prehistoric times up to the present day*, ed. Harald Hvarfner, pp. 159–88. Stockholm: Norrbottens Museum.

———. 1956. The story of the bear wife in Nordic tradition. *Ethnos* 21: 37–56.

Etter, C. 1949. *Ainu folklore*. Chicago: Wilcox and Follett.

Ewers, J. C. 1955. The bear cult among the Assiniboin and their neighbors of the northern plains. *Southwestern J. of Anthropology* 11 (1): 1–14.

Gill, S. D. 1982. *Native American religions: an introduction*. Belmont, Calif.: Wadsworth.

Gimbutas, M. 1989. *The language of the goddess*. San Francisco: Harper and Row.

———. 1974. *The goddesses and gods of old Europe*. London: Thames and Hudson.

Grant, M., and J. Hazel, 1973. *Who's who in classical mythology*. London: Weidenfeld and Nicolson.

Gubernatus, A. de. 1872, 1968. *Zoological mythology, or the legends of animals*. Detroit: Singing Tree Press.

Hallowell, A. I. 1926. Bear ceremonialism in the northern hemisphere. *American Anthropologist* 28 (1): 1–75.

*Herrero, S. 1985. *Bear attacks: their causes and avoidance*. New York: Nick Lyons Books.

———. 1978. A comparison of some features of the evolution, ecology and behavior of black and grizzly/ brown bears. *Carnivore* 1 (1): 7–17.

*———, ed. 1972. *Bears—their biology and management*. Proceedings of the Second International Conference on Bear Research and Management, University of Calgary, November 1970. IUCN Publications new series no. 23.

Herrero, S., and D. Hamer. 1977. Courtship and copulation of a pair of grizzly bears, with comments on reproductive plasticity and strategy, *J. Mammalogy* 58 (3): 441–44.

*Hummel, M., ed. 1989. *Endangered spaces: the future for Canada's wilderness*. Toronto: Key Porter.

Ingram, J. 1989. *The science of everyday life*. New York: Viking.

Interagency Grizzly Bear Committee. 1987. *Grizzly bear compendium*. Available from Grizzly Bear Recovery Coordinator, U. S. Fish and Wildlife Service, Missoula, Mont.

Kitagawa, J. M. 1961. Ainu bear festival (Iyomante). *History of religions* 1: 95–151.

Klingender, F. 1971. *Animals in art and thought to the end of the Middle Ages*. London: Routledge and Kegan Paul.

Knight, R. R., and L. L. Eberhardt. 1985. Population dynamics of Yellowstone grizzly bears. *Ecology* 66 (2): 323–34.

Macey, A. 1979. *Status report on grizzly bear* Ursus arctos horribilis *in Canada*. Committee on the Status of Endangered Wildlife in Canada.

*Martinka, C. J., and K. L. McArthur, eds. 1980. *Bears— their biology and management*. Proceedings of the Fourth International Conference on Bear Research and Management, Kalispell, Mont.

McCrory, W., and E. Mallum. 1988. Evaluation of the Khuzeymateen Valley as a grizzly bear sanctuary. Friends of Ecological Reserves, Victoria, B. C., unpublished report.

McCrory, W., and S. Herrero. 1987. Preservation and management of the grizzly bear in B. C. provincial parks, the urgent challenge. B. C. Parks and Outdoor Recreation Division unpublished report.

*Meslow, E. C., ed. 1983. *Bears—their biology and man- agement*. Proceedings of the Fifth International Con- ference on Bear Research and Management, Madison, Wisc., February 1980.

Miller, S. D., and W. B. Ballard. 1982a. Homing of transplanted Alaskan brown bears, *J. Wildl. Manage.* 46 (4): 869–76.

———. 1982b. Density and biomass estimates for an interior Alaskan brown bear, *Ursus arctos*, popula- tion. *Canadian Field-Nat.* 96 (4): 448–54.

Mundy, K. R. D., and D. R. Flook. 1973. *Background for managing grizzly bears in the national parks of Canada*. Canadian Wildlife Service Report Series No. 22.

*Murie. A. 1981. *The grizzlies of Mount McKinley*. U. S. Department of the Interior Scientific Monograph Series No. 14.

Novikov, G. A. 1962. *Carnivorous mammals of the fauna of the USSR*. Jerusalem: Israel Program for Scientific Translations.

Pearson, A. M. 1975. *The northern interior grizzly bear* Ursus arctos. *L.* Canadian Wildlife Service Report Series no. 34.

Peek, J. M., et al. 1987. Grizzly bear conservation and management: a review. *Wildl. Soc. Bull.* 15 (2): 160–69.

*Pelton, M. R., et al., eds. 1976. *Bears—their biology and management*. Proceedings of the Third International Conference on Bear Research and Management, Binghamton, N.Y., and Moscow, U.S.S.R., June 1974. IUCN Publications new series no. 40.

"Pendaison." *Les nouvelles ours* 14: 13, edité par Groupe Ours Pyrénées.

Rennicke, J. 1987. *Bears of Alaska in life and legend*. Boulder, Colo.: Roberts Rinehart.

Rensberger, B. 1977. *The cult of the wild*. Garden City, N. Y.: Anchor Press/Doubleday.

Rogers, L. 1919. Home, sweet-smelling home. *Natural History* 98: 61–67.

*Russell, A. 1967. *Grizzly country*. New York: Alfred A. Knopf.

Sapir, E. 1939. Songs for a Comox dancing mask. *Ethnos* 4 (2): 49 ff.

Schoen, J. W., S. D. Miller, and H. V. Reynolds III. 1987. Last stronghold of the grizzly. *Natural History* 96: 50–60.

Servheen, C. 1987. Suggestions on the management and research needed to assure the continued existence of the brown bear in the Pyrenees. Unpublished report.

Shepard, P. 1983. The Ark of the Mind. *Parabola* 8 (3): 54–59.

*Shepard, P., and B. Sanders. 1985. *The sacred paw: the bear in nature, myth, and literature.* New York: Viking/Penguin.

Singer, F. J., and J. B. Beattie. The controlled traffic system and associated wildlife responses in Denali National Park. *Arctic* 39 (3): 195–203.

Speck, F. G., and J. Moses. 1945. *The celestial bear comes down to earth: the bear sacrifice ceremony of the Munsee-Mahican in Canada as related by Nekateit.* Reading, Pa., Public Museum and Art Gallery Sciences Publication no. 7.

Steward, J. H. 1932. A Uintah Ute bear dance, March 1931. *American Anthropologist* n. s. 34: 263–73.

Stonorov, D. 1972. Protocol at the annual brown bear fish feast. *Natural History* 81: 66ff.

Storer, T. I., and L. P. Tevis, Jr. 1955. *California grizzly.* Los Angeles: University of California Press.

Struzik, E. 1988. Seeking sanctuary. *Nature Canada* 17 (1): 13–20.

Toynbee, J. M. C. 1973. *Animals in Roman life and art.* Ithaca, N. Y.: Cornell University Press.

Turbak, G. 1984. Lord of the Mountain. *Equinox* 3(6): 63–77.

U. S. Fish and Wildlife Service. 1982. *Grizzly Bear Recovery Plan,* prepared in conjunction with the Montana Department of Fish, Wildlife, and Parks.

Vries, A. de. 1974. *Dictionary of symbols and imagery.* Amsterdam: North-Holland Publishing Co.

Zachrisson, I., and Iregren, E. 1974. *Lappish bear graves in northern Sweden: an archaeological and osteological study.* Stockholm: Early Norland 5.

*Zager, P. , ed. 1987. *Bears—their biology and management.* Proceedings of the Seventh International Conference on Bear Research and Management, Williamsburg, Virginia, and Plitvice Lakes, Yugoslavia, February and March 1987.

*———. 1985. *Bears—their biology and management.* Proceedings of the Sixth International Conference on Bear Research and Management, Grand Canyon, Arizona, February 1983.

Index